MW01134477

This book is
shared by Daddy and

. . . .

Date:

. . . .

DADDY
AND ME

B&H kids
Nashville TN

WRITTEN BY ALYSSA JONES

CONTENTS

INTRODUCTION

Young children love to crawl into Daddy's lap and read a book, hear a story, and talk about their day. Tucked in your arms, your child feels safe in a world that is new, confusing, and exciting. *Daddy and Me* is a devotional for any father who wants to spend some of these precious moments with their kids focusing on God.

This devotional time will look different for all families. Some children may be more receptive in the morning, others at bedtime, and others before dinner. Whatever the case, *Daddy and Me* is a resource to help you introduce your child to foundations of the faith in a conversational and fun way. Ultimately, this devotional is meant to help you and your child connect over the most important thing in the world: your relationship with God!

How to Use This Devotional

This book is divided into ten themes, and each theme includes ten devotions. You are free to read straight through or skip around, selecting devotions that might connect with your child on a given day.

Each devotion includes a Scripture, short thought, and prayer to share with your child, as well as a "Thoughts for Daddy" section for you. All of us—whether we are three years old, thirty-nine years old, or ninety-three years old—have more to gain from Scripture!

In the back of the book, you'll find pages for recording your favorite "daddy and me" moments as you and your child read through the devotional together. Look back over these in the future to rediscover your child's spiritual interests and what conversations you enjoyed together.

Finally, the "Big Bible Words for Me" section is a handy glossary for explaining spiritual words and concepts to your child. Remind your child (and yourself) that we will never know everything about God, but He will always help us grow in our understanding and wisdom.

More than anything, we hope *Daddy and Me: 100 Devotions to Share* provides special opportunities for you and your child to bond spiritually. May God give you the time and help you need as you shepherd your little one!

"My thoughts are not your thoughts, and your ways are not my ways." This is the LORD's declaration. "For as heaven is higher than earth, so my ways are higher than your ways, and my thoughts than your thoughts."
—Isaiah 55:8–9

WHO IS GOD?

Learning about who God is and what He is like is one of the most important things we can do! God is like us in some ways and He is unlike us in others. Because we are made in God's image, we can love others, create beauty, and do what is right. Unlike God, we cannot be everywhere at once, always make the best decision, and know all things past, present, and future. Because God is different and perfect, He is worthy of our worship.

Knowing God's qualities helps us understand who we are as people. We are creatures God dearly loves and treasures. We are also small and limited; we must depend on our awesome God for life, breath, and everything we have! In this section, we'll discover how amazing God is and see what impact His character has on our lives today.

GOD THE CREATOR

Everything was created by him,
in heaven and on earth.
—*Colossians 1:16*

What are your favorite things to look at when we go outside? At night, we count the twinkling stars and gaze at the moon. In the daytime, the bright sun shines in the sky while the tall trees stretch their branches into the air. The birds chirp lovely songs, and the grass pokes up through the dirt.

The Bible says that God made everything in heaven and on earth! Isn't that amazing? God made flowers, animals, clouds, and people. All of creation shows that God is powerful and creative. God is like an artist! He made the whole world, including you and me.

Father God, You are the Creator of everything.
Thank You for making such a wonderful world!
Help us see and enjoy everything You have made
and remember how great You are. Amen.

THOUGHTS FOR DADDY

Have you taken time recently to stop and notice God's beauty on display around you? Admire the colors in a sunset. Smell the scent of fresh herbs in a garden. Taste the sweetness of ripe fruit. Thank the Lord for His creation and then consider how you might reflect His creativity as an image bearer. For adults, life often feels too busy to be creative. But when you do find the time, what form of creativity brings you the most joy? Building, designing, cooking, playing, writing? Consider how you might worship and reflect our Creator God through your own innovation and creation.

GOD MADE ME!

It was you who created my inward parts;
you knit me together in my mother's womb.
—Psalm 139:13

Look at you! See how your toes can wiggle and your hands can clap. Did you know that God—who made the sun, the stars, the trees, and the whole world—made you too?

Before Daddy and Mommy first thought of you, God knew you. He knew your name, where you would live, and what foods you would like to eat. God decided what your skin and hair would look like. He knew what you would do for fun. God made you just the way He wanted, and He loves you very much! You are so special to me and you are so special to God.

Father God, thank You for making [child's name]. You created the whole world, and You created people with a special purpose. Help us remember You and love You with our whole hearts. Amen.

THOUGHTS FOR DADDY

Can you remember when you first held your child in your arms? Maybe you held his tiny hand in yours and watched him sleep, or maybe you felt her soft, newborn skin and admired her eyelashes. You love your child so much!

God designed your child for a specific purpose, and the same is true for you. You are no accident. Sometimes we forget this as adults, thinking that this truth is just important for kids to know. But God has a plan for the way He made you, even the imperfections. Remember that His love for you is far greater than your deep love for your child.

3

SO, SO GOOD

The LORD is good to everyone;
his compassion rests on all he has made.
—Psalm 145:9

What are some things that are *good*? Well, when God made the world, He said it was *good*. The Bible also says God is good. God made the world and all of the *good* things in it—like pets, friends, and delicious foods. Like prayers, songs, and families.

God is always good, and there is nothing bad in Him. Because of sin, there are many bad things in the world—like sickness, heartache, and death. But God can use terrible things for our good. Even when there is bad in us and around us, we can trust God because *He is good.*

Father God, when You made everything, You saw that it was good. You are so good, and You are good to us. Help us trust You at all times. Amen.

THOUGHTS FOR DADDY

Read Genesis 3:1–5. When Satan tempted Eve in the garden of Eden, what attribute of God did he question? *God's goodness.* Satan wanted Eve to doubt that God was good. He wanted her to think that God might not want the best for her.

Anytime we are tempted to sin, our faith in God's goodness is tested. Anytime we see pain and suffering, we are tempted to wonder if God knows what's best. When you notice evil in the world—and even sin inside yourself—do you doubt God's goodness? Confess your doubt. Remember the Enemy's schemes, and look to Jesus to help you fight temptation.

4

LOVING THE WHOLE WORLD

"The Father himself loves you, because you
have loved me and have believed
that I came from God."
—John 16:27

Can you think of people who love you? Daddy loves you. Who else loves you? Mommy, grandmas, grandpas, aunts, uncles, cousins, brothers, sisters, teachers, friends, neighbors, and more. So many people know you and love you! Most of all, God loves you. People are important to God. He made all people, He has a wonderful plan for them, and He wants everyone to know Him.

God loves the whole world, and nothing we do will change that love. Nothing—not life, death, heights, depths, or powers in heaven or on earth—will be able to separate us from God's great love (Romans 8:38–39).

Father God, You made all people and You love us. Thank You for giving us family and friends who love us and whom we can love. Amen.

THOUGHTS FOR DADDY

God loves people! How do we know this? He promised Abraham that He would bless the whole world through Abraham's family (Genesis 12:1–3). Then God kept His promise by sending Jesus.

Look at Revelation 7:9. God's family will be filled with people from every nation, tribe, people, and language. The good news is that God's love isn't only for people who have it all together. God loves the undeserving, the broken, and the rebellious. His love saves us from ourselves. Have you depended on the love of God recently? Do you trust that love is for all kinds of people, including yourself?

NO BEGINNING, NO END

When is your birthday? On your birthday, we celebrate the day you were born! Now that you've entered the world, you grow day by day, a bit more each year.

What about God? Does He have a birthday? Nope. No one ever made God; He has always existed. The Bible says God has always been, even before He created the world. And guess what else? God lives forever! He will never die. God has no beginning and no end. This is one way God is very different from us. Isn't He amazing?

Father God, You were there in the beginning and You will be there in the end. We trust You because You are so big! We love You. Amen.

THOUGHTS FOR DADDY

Read Revelation 1:17–18. Because Jesus Christ is the First and the Last, we don't have to worry about what might happen to us in the seventy or eighty years we have on earth. Our lives are but a wisp, a passing shadow, a breath—but Christ's life endures forever.

When we trust in Jesus and receive forgiveness and eternal life, we have nothing to fear on earth. A life lived for God will last forever. Do you believe that today? What fear do you need to take to the One who calls Himself "the Living One"?

STRONG AND MIGHTY

Jesus looked at them and said, "With man this is impossible, but with God all things are possible."
—Matthew 19:26

How strong are you? Can you show me your muscles? Wow! Now, considering your strength, do you think you would be able to make a mountain? Could you stop a river from flowing? Could you knock down the tall walls around a city? No?

Well, these are things *God* has done. God is so strong and powerful; He can do anything! Compared to God, you and I are weak. But the Bible says God can make us strong when we put our trust in Him. Nothing is too hard for God.

Father God, You are strong and mighty!
You have done amazing things. When we
feel frustrated because we cannot do something,
remind us to look to You for help. Amen.

THOUGHTS FOR DADDY

It's natural for fathers to want to protect their children. In the same way, God the Father desires to protect us. God always uses His strength for good.

What interactions have you had in the past with people in positions of power? Were they positive or negative? People sometimes use power for evil. But God always uses His power for good—to create, protect, bring peace, and save. Even in our limited strength, God calls us to look after the weak and vulnerable. God's power is displayed through us. How have you displayed your power lately? Has it been in a way that glorifies God?

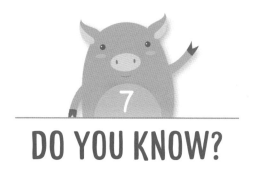

7

DO YOU KNOW?

Our Lord is great, vast in power;
his understanding is infinite.
—Psalm 147:5

You know so many things! You've learned so much already: your colors, your animals, and your ABCs. As you grow, you will learn more and more.

Did you know that God does not need to learn anything? He knows everything already! God knows how many hairs are on your head. He knows when a bird falls to the ground. He knows everything that is happening now and everything that will happen in the future. He knows how you are feeling and what you are thinking. You can talk to God about anything and trust Him to lead you in life.

Father God, You know all things! We praise You because You know everything that is happening in the world, and You know everything about us. Amen.

THOUGHTS FOR DADDY

"Daddy, how do you file taxes?" You've likely never heard this question from your preschooler. But even if you did, you probably wouldn't try to answer it; such knowledge is beyond the grasp of a child.

What leaves you feeling confused? Does your lack of understanding ever make you feel inadequate? As adults, we are not that different from our children, with finite brains and limited knowledge. God, on the other hand, knows everything, and He doesn't burden us with what we don't need to know. Don't let your lack of knowledge lead to anxiety. Instead, trust in God who, in His perfect wisdom, holds all things together.

HERE, THERE, EVERYWHERE

Where can I go to escape your Spirit?
Where can I flee from your presence?
—Psalm 139:7

Are we at school right now? Are we at the zoo? Are we at home? We can only be in one place at a time. Where is your favorite place to be?

I can't always be with you. But no matter where you are, your heavenly Father, God, is there too. We can't see God, but the Bible says God is in all places at all times (Jeremiah 23:24). That means you are never alone. Whether you're having a good or bad day, God is there. When you need help or someone to talk to, God is there. He is with you everywhere!

Father God, You are everywhere! You are even here with us right now. Help us remember that we are not alone when we feel afraid. Amen.

THOUGHTS FOR DADDY

God is omnipresent, or fully present in all places at all times. He is aware of everything going on in the world, from global pandemics to family conflict to your own thoughts and concerns. Not only is He aware of them, but He cares deeply about these things.

Does that feel true in your life? Or do you feel distant from and unseen by God? Read Jeremiah 23:23–24. You may not always be aware of God's presence, but you can trust that He is near and will answer when you call to Him. Our God holds the entire universe together by the power of His word, and He will never let you out of His sight.

HOLY, HOLY, HOLY

"I am the LORD, who brought you up from
the land of Egypt to be your God,
so you must be holy because I am holy."
—Leviticus 11:45

Out of all of your toys, is there one that is the most special to you? Maybe you set it apart from the rest of your toys and keep it in a different place. That toy is not like any of your other toys!

The Bible says that God is *holy*. Have you ever heard that word before? *Holy* means "set apart." This means there is no one like God. He is completely special, good, and right. God wants us to be holy, or set apart, like Him. How do we do that? We start by following Jesus. As we get to know Jesus, He changes us by His Holy Spirit and makes us more like Him.

Father God, You are holy! No one is like You, and You are always good and true. We want to be holy like You, so help us learn what You are like and change us. Amen.

THOUGHTS FOR DADDY

Out of all of God's attributes, the Bible puts the greatest emphasis on His holiness. Read Isaiah 6:3. God is holy, holy, holy. God's holiness can be described as His purity and righteousness, or His otherness.

Is *holy* a word you would use to describe yourself? God calls believers to be holy (Leviticus 19:2; 1 Peter 1:16). We become holy as we get to know Jesus more. Meditating on how Jesus lived on earth, we can reflect His attitude and actions by the power of His Spirit in us. Do you desire to be holy, or other, like Christ? Are you tempted to fit in with the world?

IT'S NOT FAIR!

The LORD loves justice and will
not abandon his faithful ones.
—Psalm 37:28

Have you ever thought, *That's not fair!*? Maybe someone got a cookie and you didn't. Or maybe someone got to play with a toy longer than you did. We all want things to be fair, don't we?

The Bible says that God is fair and just. He always does what is right. God made you, and He gave you that sense of wanting what is right to happen. We see lots of unfair things in the world right now. But one day Jesus will set up His perfect kingdom on earth and make all the wrong things right. While we wait for that day, we do what we can to stand up for what is right.

Father God, we cry out to You because we see unfairness all around us. Help us stand up for what is right and bring peace that comes from Jesus to this earth. Amen.

THOUGHTS FOR DADDY

God created us with a desire for justice. We want wrongdoers to be punished. We want our good deeds to be rewarded. God calls us to seek justice in the world and to stand up for those who are vulnerable.

What acts of injustice have you witnessed or experienced yourself? Do you hesitate to believe that God will keep His promise to punish the wicked? Think of people in your community who are victims of injustice. Ask God to help you fight for what is good, and while you do, keep trusting Him to one day make all things right.

God is not a man, that he might lie, or a son of man, that he might change his mind. Does he speak and not act, or promise and not fulfill?
—*Numbers 23:19*

GOD'S PROMISES

When someone says, "I promise," what does he mean? He's asking you to trust his words and believe he will do exactly what he says. Sadly, sometimes people break their promises. What they promised to do may never happen. This can be really disappointing—especially if the promise was for a delicious ice cream cone!

Did you know the Bible is full of God's *promises*? That means it's full of truths we can trust with our whole hearts. Whatever God says will always come true! Because we are so small and God is so big, we might not see *how* God is keeping His promises, or we might not know *when* they will come true. But if God said it, we can believe it. God's word can never be broken! In this section, we'll learn about some of the promises God makes in the Bible.

GOD PROMISES TO BE WITH YOU

The LORD is good, a stronghold in a day of distress.
—Nahum 1:7

What makes you feel afraid? Sometimes thunderstorms can be scary. What about being alone? Or being in the dark?

As your daddy, I will do everything I can to keep you safe. But even when I am not with you, you have a heavenly Father who promises to always be with you. When you worry, you can pray to God. The Bible tells us that He is in control of all things; He can calm a storm or shine light into dark places. When something is troubling you, tell Him how you feel and ask Him to protect you. We can trust God when we are afraid.

Father God, when we are afraid,
please comfort and protect us. You are good
and in control of all things. Help us trust in You.
Amen.

THOUGHTS FOR DADDY

How do we calm a child's fear of the dark? Often, by turning on a lamp or nightlight, exposing the unknown. Fear arises when we are uncertain about something or realize something is out of our control. As adults, we tend to grow out of being afraid of the dark, but we are still fearful. We wonder, *What will happen if I lose my job?* Or, *What if I get sick? Will my children turn out okay?*

We don't know what will happen tomorrow, but we know the One who does. Not only is He aware of the future, He promises to remain in control of it. Everything God does is for His glory and our ultimate good.

GOD PROMISES TO HELP

My help comes from the LORD,
the Maker of heaven and earth.
—Psalm 121:2

When God made people and gave them a home on the earth, He took care of them. He still takes care of us today. One way God helps us is by putting people in our lives who are helpers. Do you know any helpers? Who helps you put on your shoes? Who helps you make cookies or brush your teeth?

When you can't do something, you can ask for help. If you feel worried or upset, you can pray with faith, and God promises to hear it. God also wants us to show love to others by helping them! Who do you know who might need your help?

Father God, You are strong. You love us and want to help us. Help us be quick to ask for Your help and to help others. Amen.

THOUGHTS FOR DADDY

Asking for help is humbling. It requires us to set aside pride and confess that we lack strength or knowledge. There is no shame in admitting a need.

Read John 14:13–14. God is eager to help when we ask. Be aware of the ways God helps His people. The Bible shows us that sometimes God intervenes directly. For example, He helped Peter escape from prison. Sometimes He doesn't intervene, like when Paul asked for the thorn in his flesh to be removed. Sometimes God gives us other people to help us. Keep an eye out for how God might be sending aid, and do not be too proud to receive it.

GOD PROMISES TO NEVER LIE

It is impossible for God to lie.
—Hebrews 6:18

Have you ever told a lie? Why do you think people might lie? Maybe they did something wrong or they feel embarrassed. When people lie, they want others to think something is true even though it's not.

The Bible says that God does not lie; in fact, it's impossible for Him. When God says He will do something, He will definitely do it. It's a promise! God tells us, in the Bible, what is true about everything—about Himself, about the world, and about people. We can trust God because He always tells the truth! God wants us, as His children, to speak the truth also.

Father God, You always tell the truth, so we can trust You completely. Thank You for doing what You say You will do. Help us be truthful too. Amen.

THOUGHTS FOR DADDY

Think about the last time you told a lie. Were you trying to protect your reputation? Maybe someone else's reputation? Were you trying to escape unwanted consequences?

Read Colossians 3:9–10. Jesus invites us into a new way of living. He calls us out of the darkness of deceit and into the light of righteousness. You don't have to be afraid of being truthful before God; He already knows everything about you, and He loves you. Spend time in prayer, confessing anything you have been trying to hide from Him, and ask God for courage to walk in the light—both with Him and in front of other people.

GOD PROMISES
TO KEEP WORKING

*He who started a good work in you will carry it on
to completion until the day of Christ Jesus.
—Philippians 1:6*

How do you feel when you start working and have to stop before you are finished? Maybe you've had to stop coloring a picture because it was time for dinner. Or maybe you've had to stop building a tower because it was time for bed. Stopping in the middle of something can be really frustrating!

The Bible tells us that God is at work in the world today, both in creation and in our hearts. Do you think God ever gets tired or distracted and stops working? No way! God promises to change the hearts of those who trust in Jesus, and God never stops doing what He says He will do.

Father God, You did not make us and then leave us on our own. You are with us, helping us. As we grow day by day, change us to be like Jesus. Amen.

THOUGHTS FOR DADDY

Think about what you were like before you trusted in Jesus. What has changed since then? The Christian life is a process of sanctification, or becoming more like Jesus. Sometimes that process feels frustratingly slow, especially when you become increasingly aware of your sin.

Does it ever feel like God isn't working in your life? Do you think your thoughts or attitudes will never change? Keep your eyes open to ways in which God is working. Don't dismiss blessings as simple good luck or unexpected provision as mere coincidence. God is at work in the world, and He's still at work in you. Consider what He's been up to lately.

15

GOD PROMISES TO GIVE US REST

"Come to me, all of you who are weary
and burdened, and I will give you rest."
—Matthew 11:28

Did you know God created us to need rest? When we are tired, we snuggle up in bed and go to sleep. Sleeping gives our bodies a chance to rest, heal, and grow.

God promises to give us a different kind of rest too—rest for our hearts. God loves us and accepts us when we trust in Jesus, so following Jesus means we have a safe place with God. We don't have to figure out how to make God happy or get Him to love us. Those who trust in Jesus receive the Holy Spirit and join God's forever family. With Him, we can find true rest.

Father God, You never sleep. You never need to rest, but we do. Help us trust You as we rest our bodies. Give us rest for our hearts in Jesus. Amen.

THOUGHTS FOR DADDY

What is your dream vacation spot? Imagine resting in that place with no deadlines or responsibilities, ideal weather, and a wide-open agenda. A place like that could provide some relaxation and rest, at least for a little while. Then it's back to the daily grind of parenting, work, finances, and more.

Is there anything apart from God you turn to in order to find rest? When Jesus invites us to come to Him for rest, He doesn't promise ease or luxury. He promises that among the pressures and worries of the world, we will find unconditional love, acceptance, and peace—rest for a weary heart—in Him.

GOD PROMISES TO COMFORT US

You will keep the mind that is dependent on
you in perfect peace, for it is trusting in you.
—Isaiah 26:3

When you feel sad, what makes you feel better? A
hug from a favorite stuffed animal or someone you
love? Taking a deep breath? Crying into your pillow?
I wish we could be happy all the time, but because
of sin, sad things do happen in the world. Still, God
promises to comfort us.

God does not promise to take the pain away, but
He does promise to give us joy and hope no matter
what is going on. God's comfort is special; it only
comes from heaven. When other people are upset,
we can show them the same comfort God gives us.
We can listen, hug them, and pray for them.

Father God, You know when we are sad.
Thank You for comforting us and giving us
hope no matter what. Teach us how to comfort
others and show them Your love. Amen.

THOUGHTS FOR DADDY

Have you been grieving something difficult recently? Grief was not a foreign concept to people in the Bible. Think of how Jesus' disciples must have felt when He was crucified and sealed behind a tomb. Yet three days later Jesus rose from the dead! After doing so, Jesus comforted His disciples with His presence, forgiveness, and Holy Spirit.

Grief is not something to be avoided as adults. The world is not as it should be. Because of sin, things have gone very badly and will continue to do so. But as Christians, we can have enduring hope and peace in all circumstances, including in our grief. We hold on to the hope that God is in control and that He comforts those who come to Him.

GOD PROMISES TO BE STRONG FOR US

*"My grace is sufficient for you,
for my power is perfected in weakness."*
—2 Corinthians 12:9

Can you think of a time when you tried to do something, but it was too hard? Maybe you had trouble putting on your coat. Or maybe you could not lift a heavy box. What did you do? Did you ask for help? Even I sometimes have trouble doing things on my own.

The Bible says that we are weak, but God is strong. God promises to help those who tell Him about their struggles. How do you think God helps us? Sometimes He gives us courage to be brave, or wisdom to know what to do. Other times He sends other people to help, like a parent, teacher, or sibling. God wants to use you to help others too!

Father God, strength and power come from You. When we feel frustrated about something we can't do, help us remember that help comes in all kinds of ways. Help us be quick to help others too! Amen.

THOUGHTS FOR DADDY

Recognizing our neediness is a mark of maturity and humility. Read Mark 2:17. Jesus didn't come for people who think they have it all together. He came for needy sinners. Our weaknesses and dependency are, ironically, great sources of strength. They lead us to put our faith in Jesus and rely on community instead of doing everything ourselves.

How do you react when you can't do something? Do you get angry, overwhelmed, bitter? God's power works through those who are open to His help, and He is glorified through us when we rely on Him and others. Ask God to help you view your weakness as a means to bring Him greater glory.

18

GOD PROMISES
TO NEVER LEAVE US

"Do not fear, for I am with you; do not be afraid,
for I am your God. I will strengthen you."
—Isaiah 41:10

Who is your favorite friend to play with? You have a lot of fun together! When it's time to stop playing, how do you feel when you have to say goodbye?

Did you know you have a Friend who never leaves you? That's right—God! You never have to say goodbye to Him. You never have to wonder if He likes you. If you are afraid, God is there. If you need to confess a sin, He will forgive you right away. If you want to ask for something, He will hear. God will always tell you the truth. He will never lead you astray.

Father God, You are here with us. Help us feel Your presence. Give us joy and peace in our hearts. Thank You for never leaving us. Amen.

THOUGHTS FOR DADDY

Who do you enjoy spending your free time with most? What do you love about this friend? Why is their presence such a comfort for you?

Read Psalm 16:11. The Bible says that in God's presence, there is abundant joy. Do you see God as a Friend? If not, why not? Do you have a plan to regularly spend time with Him, both through His Word and in prayer? If you've dedicated time to this in the past, you know from experience that you won't regret it. In God's presence, there is more fulfillment and happiness than with anyone else.

GOD PROMISES HE WILL WIN

He will wipe away every tear from their eyes. Death will be no more; grief, crying, and pain will be no more, because the previous things have passed away.
—Revelation 21:4

Is there a movie you like to watch? What happens in it? Some of the most exciting movies have a problem character, like a villain. The good guy tries to stop the bad guy. And who usually wins? The good guy!

The Bible tells us that Jesus died on the cross. At the time, it seemed like the bad guys won. But three days later, Jesus rose from the dead and is alive! God promises that one day He will defeat evil forever. Jesus will come back and make all the bad things go away. God promises the greatest good guy, Jesus, will win!

Father God, no matter what bad things happen in the world, we know that You are good. And You promise to work all things together for good. We look forward to the day when Jesus comes back! Amen.

THOUGHTS FOR DADDY

Why is there still so much suffering in the world? Why do people still die? If God is in control, why is there evil at all? Life in a world wrecked by the curse of sin leaves us groaning for relief. We sometimes wonder if God even cares.

Read Hebrews 9:28. The Bible says God is waiting, but one day He will come back. God will punish people who are against Him and send them away, and He will comfort everyone who follows Him. Evildoers will always get what they deserve; justice is promised. Take heart! Jesus is coming.

GOD PROMISES TO KEEP ALL HIS PROMISES

The Lord does not delay his promise, as some
understand delay, but is patient with you.
—2 Peter 3:9

Isn't it hard to wait for something you really want?
When you get presents for your birthday or at
Christmas, you want to open them right away! But
what if you were making brownies? Would you want
to take them out of the oven after ten seconds?
No! Undercooked brownies would be terrible to eat.
When we are patient and wait for the brownies to
finish baking, we can enjoy a delicious dessert!

In the Bible, Jesus promised that He would come
back one day. But why doesn't He come right now?
The Bible says God is patient. One day is like a
thousand years to Him! There are some promises
we have not seen come true yet, but we can rely on
God to keep all His promises.

Father God, You are good, and Your timing is always perfect. Help us trust You as we wait for You to keep Your promises. Thank You for keeping Your promise to send Jesus! Amen.

THOUGHTS FOR DADDY

Are you a wait-and-see person or more of a get-it-done person? In a world where delayed gratification is a thing of the past, trusting God's timing can be challenging. Doesn't it feel empowering to make things happen on our own?

Yet, when circumstances are out of our control, we must wait on God. In the waiting, we don't always understand what is going on, but we can model faith and trust in Jesus in how we wait. God's timing is perfect. His patience is long-suffering. Are you tempted to demand things exactly as you want them? If so, what does your attitude say to your children about what (or rather, who) you believe in?

[Jesus] is the image of the invisible God, the firstborn over all creation. For everything was created by him, in heaven and on earth, the visible and the invisible, whether thrones or dominions or rulers or authorities—all things have been created through him and for him.
—*Colossians 1:15-16*

WHO IS JESUS?

Jesus is the Son of God. He's the most important person who ever lived. More than two thousand years ago, Jesus came to earth from heaven to show us God's glory and love for us by dying for sinners.

Being the Son of God means that Jesus knows exactly what it's like to live on earth, but He never did anything wrong. It also means even though Jesus has power over everything, He allowed evil people to beat up and kill Him. Jesus gave up His life for us and then, three days later, rose from the dead. No one else has ever done this, and no one else will do it again. Jesus is special. He is God—perfectly good and entirely powerful. Those who want to understand what God is like can look to Jesus. In this section, we'll learn more about our wonderful Savior and Lord, Jesus.

GOD'S ONE AND ONLY SON

"God loved the world in this way: He gave his one and only Son, so that everyone who believes in him will not perish but have eternal life."
—John 3:16

God gave you a family. Who is in your family? A family knows one another and loves one another. Did you know that when Jesus came to earth as a baby, God gave Him an earthly family? Jesus' mother was Mary, and his earthly father was Joseph. But Jesus' true Father is God.

Jesus is God's Son. God the Father loves His Son like no one else. So when God sent Jesus to earth to pay the price for our sins by dying on the cross, He was giving up a lot. That shows how much God loves us, doesn't it? Those who trust in Jesus are brought into God's family forever!

Father God, thank You for sending Jesus,
Your one and only Son, to rescue us from sin
and bring us into Your family. Help us show
love to our family and friends. Amen.

THOUGHTS FOR DADDY

Jesus is the Son of God. Think about that for a minute. He walked on this earth, shared meals with sinners, and willingly sacrificed His life for us.

Followers of other religions focus largely on adhering to rules or practices to earn God's favor and blessing. This is what makes the gospel of Jesus such radically good news. Christians don't spend their lives trying to be accepted by God. We don't have to work our way up to heaven, because Jesus came down to us.

How does having God's acceptance change things for you in how you lead your family, do your job, treat your neighbors, make decisions, and other aspects of life? How do you feel toward God knowing He loves you as His child?

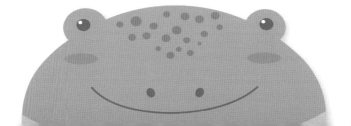

THE GREATEST KING EVER

God will bring this about in his own time.
He is the blessed and only Sovereign,
the King of kings, and the Lord of lords.
—1 Timothy 6:15

Imagine you are the king or queen of an entire kingdom for a day. What rules would you make? How would you treat other people? A king has complete control over the place where he reigns. He makes the rules and decides the punishment for people who break the rules. He is also in charge of keeping the kingdom safe from enemies.

It wouldn't be fun to live in a country with a mean king, would it? The Bible says Jesus is King over the whole earth—even over kings and other rulers. Both good and wicked rulers will come and go, but Jesus remains. He is the *best* king, and He loves us.

Father God, what a blessing it is to be under Your rule as King of the world! You are fair and good. Help us have a thankful attitude as we live for You. Amen.

THOUGHTS FOR DADDY

What kind of person do you want in charge of the country? How do you feel when someone in power acts in a way that isn't in the best interest of the community?

As long as we live on earth, we are subject to earthly authorities. Read Romans 13:1. As Christians, we submit to the government, remembering that all earthly rulers are established in God's careful sovereignty. Even in a fallen world, God can use imperfect government for His glory and to bring about good. As we live under broken earthly leadership, let's remember that our ultimate citizenship is in heaven, and we always honor God's laws first (Acts 5:29). Our true hope is in Jesus, the King of kings and Lord of lords.

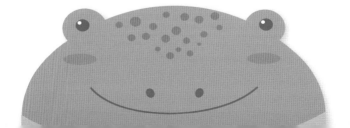

THE BEST FRIEND EVER

While he was reclining at the table
in the house, many tax collectors and sinners
came to eat with Jesus and his disciples.
—Matthew 9:10

What do you like to play with your friends? Have your friends ever not wanted to play with you? For example, maybe you wanted to color, and they wanted to build with blocks.

We can feel sad if our friends choose not to be with us. The Bible says that Jesus is a Friend to sinners. That means even the bad things about you don't keep Him from wanting to spend time with you. When Jesus was on earth, He hung out with people nobody else wanted to be with. He spent time with the rich and the poor, healthy and sick people, grown-ups and kids, and men and women. Jesus was friends with all kind of people!

Father God, thank You for friends.
Help us show love and kindness to our friends,
and give us opportunities to tell them
about Jesus—the greatest Friend ever. Amen.

THOUGHTS FOR DADDY

God is a Friend to sinners. Based on your under-standing of God, does this surprise you? Jesus being a Friend to sinners means that He draws nearer to us the more honest we are with Him.

Our sinfulness, weakness, and messy lives are exactly what qualify us to follow Jesus. The arrogant and self-righteous have no interest in befriending God. But when we humbly come to Jesus and find that He loves us in spite of our worst, we begin to open up to the work of His Spirit. Our lives begin to transform to look more like Him. Because all of us are sinners, Jesus truly is the Friend we want and the Friend we need.

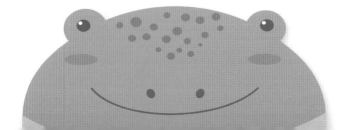

JESUS LOVES ME

We love because he first loved us.
—1 John 4:19

Did you know that before you were born, I loved you? I didn't know what you would look like, what you would be good at, or who you would become. I loved you because you are my child, a gift from God. It is not hard to love you, even when you disobey, whine, or eat all my ice cream. Do you know why? Because my love for you is so big!

Guess what? Jesus loves you like that—only better! We know this because the Bible tells us that Jesus died on the cross for you. This is the best gift of all because it means your sins can be forgiven forever.

Father God, thank You for loving us no matter what. Thank You for sending Jesus to pay the price for our sins, which is the greatest love of all. Amen.

THOUGHTS FOR DADDY

Jesus loves you. That sounds like basic teaching for children, but as adults, we must never graduate from it. This simple truth is for everyone, no matter their age or experience.

Not only does Jesus love you, He also likes you. He isn't annoyed by you or frustrated with you. The cross is the place we can look to see His love for us. Jesus willingly laid down His life according to the Father's plan, knowing full well every sin we would ever commit against Him. This love saves us from our sins once and for all, *and* it sustains us in our daily lives. This love strengthens us to do whatever God asks of us and to find true rest while doing so.

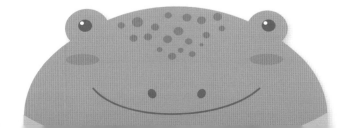

ALIVE FOREVER

This man, after offering one sacrifice
for sins forever, sat down at
the right hand of God.
—Hebrews 10:12

Jesus came to earth more than two thousand years ago. It was a much different time, with no cars, televisions, or cell phones. But people were pretty much the same back then as they are now: sinners in need of a Savior.

Jesus died on the cross to save us from our sins. Do you know what happened next? On the third day, Jesus rose from the dead! He went back to heaven, and He is alive today.

Many, many people have lived and died since then, but Jesus has remained alive, in heaven, ruling over the entire universe. Our own bodies will die one day, but everyone who trusts in Jesus will live with Him forever.

Father God, thank You for making Jesus alive again! He is stronger than death, and we look forward to the day He will return and set up His kingdom where we can live with Him forever. Amen.

THOUGHTS FOR DADDY

Numerous kings have reigned throughout history. Think of all the world leaders who have come and gone: Gandhi, Alexander the Great, Winston Churchill, Abraham Lincoln, Nelson Mandela, Mao Zedong, Cleopatra, Queen Victoria, King Richard the Lionheart, and more. These were giants of their times, but they are all gone. Even the world's most powerful leaders today will die soon.

Are you tempted to put your hope in earthly leaders? Only King Jesus is still alive. He is constant and reliable, reigning in heaven until His return. His resurrection gives us confidence in our salvation, joy for today, and hope in our future with Him forever.

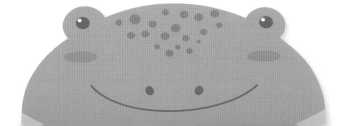

A STORY TO TELL

Do you like to listen to stories? When Jesus was on earth, He told lots of stories! Jesus' stories weren't about castles or unicorns, though. He told stories about people—like shepherds, farmers, and travelers. These stories helped people understand what God is like. For example, God is like a shepherd who looks for a lost sheep. He finds people who don't know Him and welcomes them into His family.

How did Jesus know what God is like? Because Jesus is God! Before Jesus came to earth, He lived in heaven with the Father and the Holy Spirit. We can trust what Jesus taught about God because He was teaching about Himself. One day everyone who trusts in Jesus will see God face-to-face.

Father God, thank You for sending Jesus.
Because of Him, we can know You. We want to learn
from Jesus to know what You are like. Amen.

THOUGHTS FOR DADDY

Who is the person you'd say you know best? When did you first meet? How did you get to know each other? The more time you spend with someone, the more you know him. You learn his personality, his likes and dislikes, and his hopes for the future.

The same is true with God. God reveals Himself through creation and His Word. Most of all, God showed us what He is like through Jesus. How well do you know Jesus? Not the Jesus of your imagination, but the Jesus of the Scriptures? The One who preached, served, healed, prayed, shocked, offended, and suffered? The One who gave up everything to reconcile you back to God? He is here, eager to reveal Himself to you.

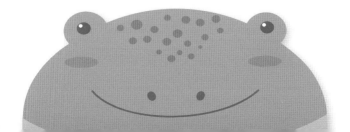

FOLLOWING RULES

We do not have a high priest who is unable to
sympathize with our weaknesses, but one who has
been tempted in every way as we are, yet without sin.
—Hebrews 4:15

What rules do we have in our house? Why is it
important to follow these rules? The rules in our
house are there to help us live together and stay
safe. Have you ever broken the rules? When we
break the rules, that's called *disobedience*. Do you
think you could follow all the rules all the time? That
would be hard to do—even for one day! Sometimes,
when we know the right thing to do, and even if we
want to do it, we still don't. We still sin.

The Bible says there is only one person who has
never, ever sinned. Can you guess who? It's Jesus!
Jesus always does what is right. Jesus always
makes the perfect choice.

Father God, we have sinned. We need to be made right with You. Thank You for Jesus, who never sinned and paid the price for us. Amen.

THOUGHTS FOR DADDY

Do you ever feel frustrated when your child struggles to obey the simplest rules? Even a rule established for a child's own good can be met with groans and grunts. As a dad, it's tempting to demand obedience from young children and expect perfect compliance. The truth is, children are sinners just like us.

Do you think God feels frustrated watching us sin over and over again? The good news is that God does not grow weary. He is patient and loving. Read Hebrews 12:5–6. God does not tolerate sin, but He lovingly disciplines and corrects us. As you parent, sympathize with your child's weakness and model true repentance, pointing to Jesus, the Friend of sinners.

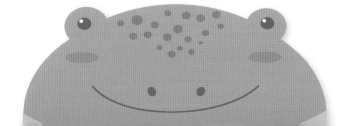

AMAZING MIRACLES

Have you ever seen something that made you say, "Wow!"? When Jesus was on earth, He amazed many people by doing miracles. Do you know what a *miracle* is? A *miracle* is something only God can do.

The Bible tells us about some of Jesus' miracles. He fed a huge crowd of people with just five loaves of bread and two fish. He healed a man with a skin disease. He made a blind man see. He raised His friend Lazarus from the dead. By doing miracles, Jesus showed His power as the Son of God. Do you know the greatest miracle Jesus ever did? He died on the cross and came back to life to save us from our sins!

Father God, You do amazing things! Best of all, You sent Jesus to die on the cross and rise from the dead to save us from our sins. Help us remember how powerful You are. Amen.

THOUGHTS FOR DADDY

Jesus' miracles are a glimpse of what the kingdom of God is like. What will God do with our suffering? How will He handle our hunger, our fears, our diseases and disabilities?

Jesus' miracles were gracious and wonderful, but His healings and signs were not the main reason Jesus came to earth. Many people watched Jesus perform miracles but did not believe He was the Son of God. They missed the whole point! Through Jesus, God did what is impossible for us to do on our own: He provided forgiveness, salvation, and eternal life for all who trust in Him. One day, we will experience life forever with God in His kingdom. What are you most looking forward to in God's kingdom?

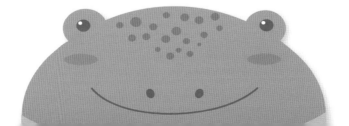

TO THE RESCUE

*This saying is trustworthy and deserving of full
acceptance: "Christ Jesus came into the world
to save sinners"—and I am the worst of them.
—1 Timothy 1:15*

Who do we call when there is a fire? Firefighters!
Who do we call when someone is hurt or sick? EMTs,
doctors, and nurses! Firefighters, EMTs, doctors,
and nurses are all *rescuers*, or people who help us
when we are in need.

The Bible says we are all in need of spiritual
rescue because our sins keep us focused on
ourselves and far away from God. What do we
need Jesus to rescue us from? Lots of things. Mean
words. Hurtful hands. Hateful thoughts. Selfish
ideas. Not doing good. Feeling pride. Jesus is our
Rescuer who saves us from all our sins when we
call out to Him.

Father God, our sin puts us in a really bad situation—
far away from You and focused on ourselves.
Sin deserves punishment, so thank You for sending
Jesus to rescue us and give us life forever. Amen.

THOUGHTS FOR DADDY

The message of Christianity is not, "You can do it! Jesus can help." We can be tempted to view Jesus not primarily as a Rescuer—saving us completely— but as a teacher or helper who guides us to do the work of earning our right standing with God.

The good news of Christianity is that Jesus does for us what we cannot do for ourselves. Read Romans 5:6. Imagine Jesus is like a lifeguard. If so, we aren't weak swimmers in need of some assis- tance; we are dead at the bottom of the lake! Jesus saves us and brings us to life. How do you tend to think about Jesus' role in your salvation? What is your response to His work?

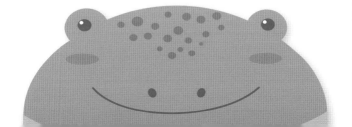

SHINE ON ME

Jesus spoke to them again: "I am the light of the world. Anyone who follows me will never walk in the darkness but will have the light of life."
—John 8:12

When it's dark at night, why should you stay in your bed? If you don't have a night-light or a flashlight, you might bump into things and get hurt!

The Bible says that Jesus is the "light of the world." What do you think that means? When we turn on a light, we see what is really in a room. So Jesus shows us what is true and real. Nothing can be hidden from Him. The Bible tells us that when we see Jesus in heaven, we won't even need the sun because He is so bright! Jesus is worth following. Without Him, we remain in the dark. We can trust in Jesus.

Father God, thank You for sending Jesus to be the Light of the world! There is no darkness in You at all. Show us how to live in a way that honors You. Amen.

THOUGHTS FOR DADDY

If you've ever found yourself experiencing a power outage as the sun sets, you know how quickly the darkness can overtake the house and make it difficult to see anything. Flip on a headlamp or light a candle, and even a small amount of light can bring peace, calm, and renewed hope.

The Bible uses this imagery to describe the world (darkness) apart from Jesus (Light). Do you ever feel like you are stumbling around in a dark and confusing world? Jesus came into the world to show us the way to the Father. He called Himself "the light of the world" (John 8:12). Look to Him for peace, calm, and renewed hope. In Him, there is no darkness at all.

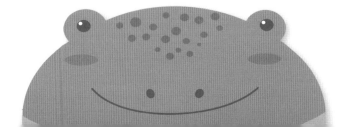

As far as the east is from the west, so far has
he removed our transgressions from us.
—Psalm 103:12

GOD'S FORGIVENESS

What is *forgiveness*? *Forgiveness* is a big word that means not getting back at someone for hurting you. The world is full of people who might hurt us—either because they intend to or by accident. People say mean things. They take what doesn't belong to them. They tell lies. They break promises. They choose to be selfish and not consider our feelings. All these things are painful, yet God can help us forgive people who hurt us.

Jesus forgives us for every sin we have ever committed. That's *big* forgiveness! When we trust in God's enormous forgiveness and God puts His love in our hearts, we have the power to forgive others over and over again. In this section, we'll learn all about God's forgiveness and how we can forgive others.

31

FROM GOD WITH LOVE

God proves his own love for us in that
while we were still sinners, Christ died for us.
—Romans 5:8

Getting gifts is always fun! People who love you sometimes give you gifts. What are some of your favorite gifts you've been given?

The Bible says that God gave us a great gift. He sent His Son, Jesus, into the world to live among us, die for us on the cross, and then rise again to reign as King forever. Jesus isn't like any other gift. He's not a toy we can play with or forget about; He is a person we can know, love, and obey. Jesus offers us a relationship with God that will change our lives forever. Isn't that an amazing gift? There's nothing we have to do to earn this gift. All we have to do is tell God we want it and receive it in faith.

Father God, thank You for loving us and for giving us the greatest gift ever: Jesus! Help us treasure Jesus more than anything else. Amen.

THOUGHTS FOR DADDY

Are you a gift person? Do you enjoy receiving gifts? Do you enjoy giving them? Why or why not? While gifts can be great ways to show love, the best gift is to give of yourself for another person. This is extremely difficult—especially when the other person is not deserving—but it represents the heart of Christ.

Read John 15:13. Think about how radical following Jesus is in a world where most people are focused on their own best interests. Christlike selfless love does not go unnoticed—at least, not by God. Spend some time thinking about the gift God gave you in Christ—the gift of His very self—and consider how you might give of yourself to those around you.

32

WE ALL FALL

All have sinned and fall short
of the glory of God.
—Romans 3:23

Can you think of a time you made a wrong choice? Maybe I told you to pick up your toys and you didn't want to, so you kept on playing instead. Or maybe you saw someone in trouble but didn't offer to help her.

When we don't do what we should, or when we do what we shouldn't do, that's called sin. The Bible says everyone *sins*, or makes wrong choices. You sin; Daddy sins; all people sin! The only person who never sinned was Jesus. When we make a wrong choice, we can say we are sorry and ask God (and the other person) for forgiveness.

Father God, we know we are sinners. We need Your help! Thank You for sending Jesus to save us. Help us make right choices that honor You. Amen.

THOUGHTS FOR DADDY

How do you feel when you've done something you know is wrong, or you refrained from doing something you know is right? When it comes to sin, we are no different from our children. We all sin. And our sin is a big deal because God is a big deal. To rebel against His holiness is no small offense. Hurting others is also a big deal because people are made in God's image.

Have you sinned against anyone lately? Ask for forgiveness from both God and that person. If you've sinned against your child, humble yourself before her and ask for forgiveness. This will go a long way in teaching your child the message that we are all sinners.

33

GOOD AND BAD CHOICES

*If we confess our sins, he is faithful
and righteous to forgive us our sins
and to cleanse us from all unrighteousness.*
—1 John 1:9

Did you know there is nothing we can do to stop God from loving us? When we make wrong choices, He keeps loving us. When we make bad choices and we even don't realize it, He keeps loving us. When we make good choices with His help, He loves us too! Because of this truth, we never need to hide from God.

In fact, Jesus died for you so that whenever you make a bad choice, you can go immediately to God, say you're sorry, and receive complete forgiveness. There is no love as big as God's love for you! It goes on forever and ever.

Father God, we are sinners, but You gladly forgive our sins! Help us be quick to come to You when we make wrong choices. We never want to hide from You. Amen.

THOUGHTS FOR DADDY

A shiny car, fresh laundry, cleared countertops. The very act of cleaning can bring a sense of relief and new beginnings.

Is there anything in your life that feels like it needs to be "cleaned up"? Don't hesitate to take it to the Lord. Nothing is shocking to Him, and nothing surprises Him. Confess what you've done (or not done). He will not greet you with disappointment, agitation, or anger. God does not grow weary of us, and He does not keep a record of wrongs against us. In Christ, He will forgive us repeatedly. So come clean before Him. Tell Him the honest truth. Thank Him for His forgiveness in Christ that is offered forever.

34

FORGIVING OTHERS

*Just as the Lord has forgiven you,
so you are also to forgive.
—Colossians 3:13*

Can you think of a time someone did something that made you feel angry or upset? Maybe a friend took away a toy you were playing with. What did you do? Sometimes people do things that hurt us, and we often want to hurt them back! But we can make another choice: we can forgive them.

Forgiving someone means choosing not to be mad for what he did to you. It means not wanting to hurt a person because she hurt you. This can be hard to do, but with God, it is possible! When we trust in Jesus, God forgives us for our sins. He puts a love in our hearts that's so big, we can forgive others like He has forgiven us.

Father God, when we trust in Jesus, You forgive our sins completely. Thank You! When others hurt us, help us forgive them just like You forgive us. Amen.

THOUGHTS FOR DADDY

Why can it be so hard to forgive? When someone wrongs you, you might feel angry or betrayed. You might want that person to pay for what he did. Often, that feeling is justified, so forgiving isn't easy. When you forgive someone who's wronged you, you choose not to demand anything from her. You choose to hand your anger and resentment over to God. This can come at great cost to yourself.

Yet, any cost we incur in forgiving others pales in comparison to what it cost God to forgive us. Jesus laid down His life and faced the Father's wrath so that every sin of ours is fully paid for. Because we've received such radical forgiveness, we can freely turn around and forgive others.

35

THE HEIGHT OF HIS LOVE

LORD, your faithful love reaches to heaven,
your faithfulness to the clouds.
—Psalm 36:5

How high is the tallest building you've ever seen? Pretty tall, huh? Do you like going up high, or do you prefer to stay on the ground? The Bible says that there is no limit to the height of God's love for us, and nothing can separate us from it (Romans 8:38–39).

Now spread your arms out wide to your sides. Imagine your left arm kept going forever and your right arm kept going forever too. Once you got to the very end, that's how far apart the Bible says God removes our sins from us (Psalm 103:12). This means that you could never do something bad enough that God won't forgive you for. Isn't that wonderful news?

Father God, thank You for Your love and forgiveness that go on forever. I trust that when I confess my sins, Your love covers them and Your forgiveness removes them. Amen.

THOUGHTS FOR DADDY

Is there a part of you that thinks God is holding your sins against you? Is there a part of you that believes you still have to make up for any wrongs you've done? When God says He removes our transgressions from us as far as the east is from the west, He is not exaggerating. They really are infinitely gone.

This forgiveness is made possible through Christ's sacrifice and atonement. To assume your sins must be paid for by both you and Jesus is arrogant at worst, ignorant at best. Trust in the gospel and find freedom from your sin. Take time today to thank Jesus for what He has truly done for you.

36

NO MORE HIDING!

There is now no condemnation
for those in Christ Jesus.
—Romans 8:1

Do you like to play hide-and-seek? What are your favorite hiding spots? Sometimes when we do wrong things, we want to hide. Did you know the Bible says that we don't have to hide from God? It's okay to feel bad for doing the wrong thing, but God wants us to come to Him and ask for forgiveness.

God knows everything, and He will always forgive us when we ask Him. Instead of trying to hide when you mess up, you can pray to God and tell Him what's going on. You can also come to me! I don't want you to hide from me either. If there's a sin to *confess*, or to admit you have done, we can talk and pray about it together.

Father God, You know us. No matter what mess we find ourselves in, we don't have to hide from You. You forgive our sin and love us. Amen.

THOUGHTS FOR DADDY

Are there people in your life who expect you to behave a certain way no matter what's going on? Maybe at work, a certain level of professionalism is expected. Maybe at church, a certain level of cordiality is expected.

Although many believe a certain level of holiness is expected before coming to God, that's not true. In Christ, God simply invites us to come—just as we are, undeserving, messy, and humble. God is a safe place to turn to in the midst of our failures, sufferings, and sins. There is no condemnation in Christ Jesus, which means that, like our children, we don't have to hide.

37

ALL IN THE FAMILY

See what great love the Father has given us that we should be called God's children—and we are!
—1 John 3:1

Who are some of your friends? Who are some of your family members? What is the difference between our friends and the people who are in our family? Family members are connected in a way that is stronger than friendship. Friends might come and go, but family members will always be part of the family.

Did you know God invites us into His family? When we trust in Jesus for forgiveness, God the Father adopts us as His children. We get a place in His house (John 14:2) and can come to Him whenever we need Him. Being in God's family is the best because He is a loving Father who protects us and gives us everything we need.

Father God, it is so amazing that You want us to be part of Your family! Thank You for inviting us to be Your children. We love You. Amen.

THOUGHTS FOR DADDY

In our sin and brokenness, we might relate to God as a servant to a master, an orphan to a guardian, or a fugitive to the authorities. But because of the grace of Christ, He has loved us into His own family and called us His children.

Learning how to walk with God as a son is one of the greatest journeys of the Christian life. Jesus said, "A slave does not remain in the household forever, but a son does remain forever" (John 8:35). Think of the love you have for your own child. God's love toward both you and your child is even greater than that!

38

FORGIVENESS FOR ALL

In him we have redemption,
the forgiveness of sins.
—Colossians 1:14

Who do you think needs Jesus? Do people who do lots of wrong things need Jesus? Yes! Do people who do lots of right things need Jesus? Yes! Do you need Jesus? Yes! Everyone needs Jesus!

God is right to be angry about sin, and He is right to punish sin. Because Jesus died on the cross for our sin, everyone who believes in Him will be forgiven. When God forgives, He does not hold our sin against us anymore; He does not keep a record of it. God's forgiveness is for everyone, and He never says no to someone who asks for forgiveness. It is a gift, so everyone who wants it can have it. Our God is pretty amazing, isn't He?

Father God, thank You that anyone can be forgiven when they ask for it. Help us be quick to come to You for forgiveness. Amen.

THOUGHTS FOR DADDY

Have you ever been tempted to think someone you know needs Jesus more than you do? Maybe a spouse or child? Maybe a neighbor or coworker?

The convicted felon and the humanitarian aid worker are both completely lost apart from Jesus. Whether your past is marked by habitual disobedience or regular righteous deeds, Jesus offers you forgiveness! The only thing God requires of you is to turn your eyes to Jesus. Even after we first believe, we can come to Him day after day with empty hands of faith. He will fill them with good gifts and forgiveness. Best of all, He will keep giving you Himself.

39

A NEW HEART

"I will give you a new heart and put
a new spirit within you; I will remove your
heart of stone and give you a heart of flesh."
—Ezekiel 36:26

What do you think of when you see a heart shape? Maybe Valentine's Day or love? Your real heart doesn't look like that. It is an organ in your chest that pumps blood to all the parts of your body. And when the Bible talks about our *hearts*, it means the part of ourselves that tells us how we feel, what we want, and what is right or wrong.

Our hearts can be tricky. Before we trust in Jesus, our hearts are like stones. Is a stone hard or soft? It's hard! A hard heart does not want to do what is right. But Jesus promises to change our hearts and make them soft. That way, we eagerly do what is pleasing to God.

Father God, You take our hard hearts and make them soft. Thank You for changing us so we can gladly do what pleases You. Amen.

THOUGHTS FOR DADDY

What was your life like before you trusted in Jesus? What changes have you noticed in your heart since you became a Christian?

The Bible describes the hearts of many kings and rulers who resisted God as being *hardened*, or refusing to listen or obey. When your heart feels hard or you feel emotions that you know are not honoring to God, take a moment to pray. Ask God to change your perspective and soften your heart. It takes humility to give up self-autonomy and live under the authority of God, but doing so is a mark of spiritual maturity. The Lord is tender with us, will always forgive us, and will not lead us astray.

40

A WAY OUT

Since he himself has suffered when he was
tempted, he is able to help those who are tempted.
—*Hebrews 2:18*

When Daddy tells you to do something, you have two choices. You can obey Daddy, or you can disobey. God says unless I am asking you to sin, obeying me is the right thing to do.

Sometimes it can feel hard to do the right thing. But God's Son, Jesus, always did the right thing. He was *tempted* by the Devil, who tried to get Him to do the wrong thing, yet Jesus always said no to temptation.

Part of growing up and following Jesus is learning that you can make the right choice, even when it feels hard. God helps us say no to temptation by giving us Jesus. Jesus knows how hard it is to do the right thing.

Father God, we want to do what is good and pleasing to You. Help us say no when we are tempted to do the wrong thing and to remember Jesus, who always does what is right. Amen.

THOUGHTS FOR DADDY

The power to resist temptation comes from Jesus. Following Jesus won't mean there's no temptation and sin in our lives. Sanctification, or becoming like Christ, is a lifelong process. We make choices every day to follow the desires of the flesh or to follow Jesus. You made choices today, and you will make choices tomorrow. The question is, *in whose power are you choosing: your own power or Christ's power?*

We are better able to resist temptation when we see Jesus as more valuable than any instant gratification and rely on His strength. When you do give into it, don't despair! We can boldly approach God's throne to receive the grace and mercy we need (Hebrews 4:16).

The precepts of the LORD are right,
making the heart glad.
—Psalm 19:8

THE BIBLE

Do you know what the Bible is? It is one big book made of sixty-six smaller books written by around forty authors over the course of fifteen hundred years. God's Spirit gave these authors the messages to write down—words that show the world what God is like, reveal His plan to save us through Jesus, and help us learn how to follow Him.

There is no book in the world as important as the Bible. That's because God uses the messages in the Bible to speak to us. Through the Bible, God helps us understand the world, understand ourselves, and live in a way that helps others and honors Him. When you read the Bible it changes your entire life! Isn't that amazing? What do you already love about the Bible? Do you want to understand the Bible more? In this section, we'll learn all about how wonderful the Bible is.

41

WHAT'S THE WORD?

All Scripture is inspired by God and is profitable for teaching, for rebuking, for correcting, for training in righteousness.
—2 Timothy 3:16

Have you ever sent a card in the mail? Or have you drawn a picture to send to someone? Letters and pictures are a few ways we send messages to people to show them that we care.

Did you know that God has given something like a letter to us? It's the Bible! The Bible is God's message to us. It tells us about His plan for the whole world through Jesus. The Bible tells us that God loves us and wants us to be in His family. It is full of exciting stories, wise guidance, and commands that come from God's heart. God is not silent; He speaks to us when we read the Bible in faith.

Father God, thank You for giving us Your words in the Bible. Grow our love for Your Word and help us understand what it says. We want to know You more! Amen.

THOUGHTS FOR DADDY

Why do we read the Bible? Because the Creator of the universe has given us a book—His own words—to teach us, guide us, and train us for life. We don't have to wonder what God is like, what matters most, or what will bring us joy. God has revealed that to us in Scripture. When you think that God is distant, pick up your Bible and listen in faith. You'll start to hear His still, small voice again.

The daunting thing is that *all* Scripture is from God: not just the parts we like—all of it. That's why we'll never outgrow the Bible; we mature and become more like Christ as we believe and practice the truth of God's Word.

42

THE WHOLE STORY

You know that from infancy you have known the sacred Scriptures, which are able to give you wisdom for salvation through faith in Christ Jesus.
—2 Timothy 3:15

If I told you that you were going to meet a new friend tomorrow, what questions would you have for me? Maybe you'd ask how old she is or what games she likes to play. You could learn a lot about a friend before you meet her!

We have never seen God face-to-face. So how do we know what is true about Him? We can read about God in the Bible! It tells us everything we need to know about God in order to trust Him. If someone tells you something about God that isn't in the Bible—like that He has purple hair or that we have to earn our way to heaven—don't believe it!

Father God, we don't have to wonder what You are like. You are mysterious, but we can know many things about You through the Bible. Thank You for Your Word. Amen.

THOUGHTS FOR DADDY

What do you currently believe about the Bible? Is it frustrating? Antiquated? Life-giving? Restoring?

The Bible is not so much an instruction manual for how to live but a *story* of who God is, what He has done for us, and what it looks like to follow Jesus in faith. It tells us about the greatest problem: our separation from God because of our sin. Then it reveals the solution: salvation through Jesus.

God is mysterious, and there's plenty about Him we cannot understand now. But He tells us everything we need to know in the Bible. The Bible is a source of encouragement, comfort, and wisdom as we follow Jesus as our Lord and Savior.

43

READ THE INSTRUCTIONS

Is it okay to hit someone? No, it's not. Is it good to tell the truth? Yes, of course! How do you know these things? God made everything, and He tells us how life works best. So we can love God by doing what the Bible says.

The Bible teaches us many things, like that God is good, God has a plan for the world, God knows our hearts, and God invites us to be like Him. The Bible also says God wants us to love one another the way He loves us. Living in these ways brings honor to God. God says if we are right with Him, we will be *blessed*, or truly happy.

Father God, thank You for telling us in Your Word how to live for You. Help us obey because we know You love us, not to earn Your love. Amen.

THOUGHTS FOR DADDY

Consider why you give your child rules. Is it to challenge her to earn your love? Of course not! We instruct our children to show them the best way of living and relating with others. We teach them because we can see the bigger picture even when they can't.

The Bible is primarily a bigger-picture story about God, but it does give us instructions for how to live as followers of Jesus. As you spend time studying your Bible, remember that God's instructions for us are not a list of requirements to earn His favor. Because we already have God's full acceptance through His Son, our response is one of obedience and love.

TRUE OR FALSE?

"Sanctify them by the truth;
your word is truth."
—John 17:17

Have you ever read a story about something that never really happened? For example, stories about unicorns are just pretend because unicorns don't really exist. But all the stories in the Bible are true! They actually happened. God's Word is truth.

What is truth? That's a big question! Well, let's start with the opposite of a truth: a lie. If I said to you, "Daddy has to work so I can't take you to the park," but I was golfing instead, I would be lying. Lies can hurt us and disappoint us. God never lies. Everything He says and promises is true, which means He will never hurt or disappoint us. We can trust everything God says in the Bible because we know His words are all true.

Father God, when we read something in the Bible, we know it is true. Thank You for giving us Your Word, the Bible. Help us understand it and trust You more every day. Amen.

THOUGHTS FOR DADDY

All the stories in the Bible are true. Believing this brings wonder to stories like God parting the Red Sea to deliver the Israelites, God providing a big fish to save Jonah, and Jesus healing people who were blind, sick, or even dead.

It can be hard to imagine that Paul was an actual person who traveled long distances to share the gospel or that Jesus' disciple Peter denied the Lord after spending three years with Him. But all these stories are there for a reason. They reveal something about God and people. What have you learned from the stories in the Bible? How have they shaped the way you follow God?

HE DID IT!

When Jesus had received the sour wine,
he said, "It is finished."
—*John 19:30*

Can you tell me all the things you did today? That might be hard since you did quite a few things! The Bible tells us some of what Jesus did while He was on earth, which was for just thirty-three years. But the Bible says that Jesus did so many things, if everything He did were written down, the whole world wouldn't be big enough to hold all the books (John 21:25).

What is the most important thing that Jesus did? Jesus died for our sins. But that's not all. God also raised Him from the dead so that He could rule forever! Jesus is alive, and He will never die again. This is the best thing He ever did.

Father God, thank You for sending Jesus to take our place and die for our sins. Thank You for raising Him from the dead. Jesus is amazing! Amen.

THOUGHTS FOR DADDY

What have you accomplished in your life? You might have medals or trophies from sports achievements, certificates recognizing outstanding work, or diplomas for completing certain levels of education. While it is good to strive for excellence, no earthly accolade will last beyond this life. Our greatest glory comes from trusting in Jesus, the One whose finished work gives us true life.

The Bible tells us all about what Jesus did. He lived the perfect life we could never live, died the death we deserve to die, and rose again to prove exactly who He was: God in the flesh. The greatest thing we could ever do is to live our lives surrendered to Him.

46

READ, READ, READ

His delight is in the LORD's instruction,
and he meditates on it day and night.
—Psalm 1:2

Imagine you sent a card to your friend. If your friend got the card and stuck it on a shelf in his room without looking at it, what would you think? That would be silly. After all, a card is meant to be read.

No matter how young or how old we are, God wants us to read His letter to us, the Bible. It is more important than any other book you will ever read! We can read the Bible every day. It is a book with stories, poems, songs, encouragements, commands, and more in it. All the words in the Bible fit together. They tell us one big story about Jesus and His love for us.

Father God, the Bible is a gift to us—a love letter showing us what You are like and how You save us through faith in Jesus. Help us understand the words when we read it. Amen.

THOUGHTS FOR DADDY

Meditating on God's Word is like chewing a perfectly cooked steak. You savor every flavor out of the bite, wishing it would last as long as possible. Meditating on the Bible will lead us to delight in who God is, what He is doing, and all that He promises us who believe in Christ.

God wants us to read the Bible. If there are parts you don't understand, pray and ask for understanding. Read commentaries or work through Bible studies. Talk with friends, mentors, or church leaders. By reading God's Word, you will taste and see that the Lord is good (Psalm 34:8).

FOR YOUNG AND OLD

I will never forget your precepts,
for you have given me life through them.
—Psalm 119:93

Some parts of the Bible can be harder to understand than others. The Bible is full of stories—some that are happy and some that are sad. It explains the laws God's people followed a long time ago and the ones we still obey today. It includes poems and songs and even letters written to the earliest churches.

Has something you heard in the Bible ever confused you? The Bible can be hard to understand, but it's always good to read. As we grow, we will understand it more and more. You can read the Bible now, in five years, and in twenty-five years. You will never be too old to read the Bible, because God always has something to teach us.

Father God, the words in the Bible are
important because they come from You.
Help us grow in our love for Your Bible and never
outgrow our desire to learn from You. Amen.

THOUGHTS FOR DADDY

Did you hear stories from the Bible as a child? What Bible stories do you like sharing with your children? As you've grown, what other parts of the Bible have you explored for your own understanding?

Teachers of the past have described Scripture like a river. Some spots are shallow, and children can play there. Other spots are deep enough for adults to swim in for long hours. The Bible is for both kids and parents, for the ordinary man and the studied theologian. You don't need a seminary degree to understand the Bible, but a seminary degree also won't make you bored of the Bible. The more time we spend reading God's Word in faith, the deeper our relationship with God can grow.

48

ALL ABOUT JESUS

"You pore over the Scriptures because
you think you have eternal life in them,
and yet they testify about me."
—John 5:39

What do you think the Bible is about? A lot of people think the Bible is a bunch of stuffy rules that make life not that fun. Yes, there are rules in the Bible, but that is not what the Bible is really about. Others think the Bible is about being like Noah, Moses, Queen Esther, and King David. Well, the Bible does tell us about those people, but that's not the main point of the Bible. After all, all those people sinned against God like we do.

In fact, the Bible is all about Jesus! Jesus is God's Son. The Bible tells us what Jesus did and how we can be saved from our sins by trusting in Him.

Father God, help us understand what we read in the Bible. Show us how the entire Bible points to Jesus. Open our eyes to see Him, and soften our hearts to love Him. Amen.

THOUGHTS FOR DADDY

Some people think the Bible is nothing more than rules for what we should and shouldn't do. In fact, the Bible is a book about a God who saves people through incarnate, sacrificial, incomprehensible love. The promises, practices, and prophets of the Old Testament point to Jesus, and the entire New Testament is about Jesus. No part of the Bible is simply about morality. It's about Jesus being the center of the universe and God's people orienting themselves around Him

For this reason, the stories in the Bible lead us beyond ourselves. The Bible is not a handbook for you living your best life. The Bible shows us that we are the problem, and Jesus is the solution. The Bible is all about Jesus.

49

REMEMBER THIS

I have treasured your word in my heart
so that I may not sin against you.
—Psalm 119:11

What is your name? Do you know when your birthday is? Can you say your ABCs? You remember so many things already! Your brain contains so much!

You can remember what the Bible says too. Try this. I'll say part of the very first verse in the Bible, and you repeat after me: "In the beginning . . . God created . . . the heavens and the earth. . . . Genesis 1:1." Great job! We can say these words again and again—we can even sing them!—to remember them. When we memorize God's Word, we can remember what is true, no matter where we are or what is going on. Let's memorize more of God's Word together.

Father God, You created us with brains to learn and remember. Help us remember what the Bible says and to love and obey You. Amen.

THOUGHTS FOR DADDY

How many Bible verses do you have memorized? Have you ever found yourself in a tough situation and a Bible verse has come to mind?

As you read the Bible, make notes of particular verses that remind you of what is true about God, your family, or yourself. Write them down on an index card or make a note in your phone. Keep the card in a place you will see several times a day, like on a mirror or dashboard. Try your hand at memorizing longer passages or even shorter books like Philippians or James. Treasure God's Word in your heart. Dwell on it. Let it sink in. Let it transform your life.

50

BREAD FOR LIFE

[Jesus] answered, "It is written: Man must not
live on bread alone but on every word
that comes from the mouth of God."
—Matthew 4:4

What is your favorite thing to eat? What foods
help your body grow strong? Making good choices
about what we eat can help us be healthy and feel
good.

Did you know the Bible helps us grow too? But
wait a second . . . you can't eat the Bible! Still, we
need more than food to live; we need God's words
found in the Bible. We don't eat the Bible, but we do
read it! The Bible helps us grow strong in our hearts
and minds. The more we believe it, the more we will
live and look like Jesus. We need the Bible to live a
healthy, full life!

Father God, just like You created us to need food, You created us to need the Bible. Give us hunger in our spirits to read the Bible every day. Amen.

THOUGHTS FOR DADDY

What is the longest time you've gone without food? How did you feel? What is the longest time you've gone without reading the Bible? How did you feel?

Like food, the Bible is necessary for life and growth. Read Deuteronomy 8:3. The longer you go without food—both physical and spiritual—the weaker you get. Make a plan to find your strength in God's Word. Spend time daily reading the Bible and praying. Notice how doing so changes how you think and feel. Your desires and goals and priorities will change. The more you spend time with God, the more you will crave it. God's Word gives us life.

The commandments, Do not commit adultery;
do not murder; do not steal; do not covet; and
any other commandment, are summed up by
this commandment: Love your neighbor as
yourself. Love does no wrong to a neighbor.
Love, therefore, is the fulfillment of the law.
—Romans 13:9-10

CREATION, COMMUNITY, AND CHURCH

After God created the first human, Adam, He put him in the garden to work it. This was a wonderful job for Adam, but then God said, "It is not good for the man to be alone" (Genesis 2:18). So God gave Adam a woman named Eve. Together, they worked the garden. Later, after they left the garden, they had children, who had more children, and all those people formed in *communities*, or groups of people who live by each other and are connected to each other. People in communities all have important jobs to do to help one another.

A *church* is a special kind of community where the group of people believes in Jesus and God's Spirit is at work. Are you part of a school or neighborhood community? Are you part of a church community? We will learn more about our roles in creation, community, and church in this section.

51

GOD MADE YOU SPECIAL

God said, "Let us make man in our image, according to our likeness. They will rule . . . the whole earth, and the creatures that crawl on the earth."
—Genesis 1:26

You have so many toys to play with. Which toys are very special to you? Out of all the things that God created—the stars, moon, plants, animals, sky, and seas—one thing God made is the most special of all. Do you know what it is? People!

People are God's special creation. When God made people, He made them different from anything else. God made people in His own image. That means God made people to be like Him in some ways. People can get wisdom like God; we can be kind and patient and loving like God too. You were made in God's image, so you are God's very special creation.

Father God, You made every person to be special.
We are not like the animals or the plants.
We can have a close relationship with You.
Thank You for giving us life. Amen.

THOUGHTS FOR DADDY

You are special to God. We tell our children this, but do you believe it? God cares about your life and what you do with it. God has a plan to fill the earth with His glory (Habakkuk 2:14), and He uses people to carry out this plan.

Being made in God's image means we are like God and represent God. When we trust in Jesus, we become temples of the Holy Spirit (1 Corinthians 6:19) and we are the aroma of Christ to the world (2 Corinthians 2:15). Because all people are made in God's image, God wants us to treat others with love and respect—even those whose hearts are far from God. All human beings have dignity. How might you live this out today?

52

CARING FOR CREATION

When God made the world, He made a garden for the first people to live in. What do you think God's garden was like? Were there beautiful flowers or thorny weeds? Do you think any animals lived there? Which ones?

The Bible tells us God's garden was beautiful. It was perfect, and the first people—Adam and Eve—loved living there. When God made people, He put them in charge of taking care of the world.

God still tells people to care for His creation today. What are some ways we can do that? We can clean up after ourselves, take care of the animals, and protect the land. Let's take care of God's creation so we can continue to enjoy it together.

Father God, You are good! You gave us an amazing planet to live on. Help us take care of Your creation and protect it. Help us see the beauty in all You made. Amen.

THOUGHTS FOR DADDY

Look at the world around you. Creation is a gift with its beautiful sunsets, snowy mountaintops, sandy beaches, and dense forests. God created the world, put people in it, and gave us dominion over it. God wants us to show care for His creation.

Think about how you—as a person made in the image of God—ought to interact with creation. God has given us the responsibility and privilege to make the world fruitful and beautiful. The earth as we know it will not last forever, but we are God's people living in God's land. How can you care for creation while we wait for the day it will be fully redeemed?

53

MADE TO CREATE!

He has filled them with skill to do all the work
of a gem cutter; a designer; an embroiderer in blue,
purple, and scarlet yarn and fine linen;
and a weaver. They can do every kind of craft.
—Exodus 35:35

What sorts of things do you like to make and build? Some kids love to build forts and block castles. Others use their imaginations to draw amazing worlds and characters. Other kids create their own songs or poems.

Why do we like to create and build? Because God made us in His image, and He is the Creator of all things. God made people to think, work, and play. When we create something amazing, we can be proud of what we've done and then remember to thank God for creating everything in the first place! We can thank Him for giving us the ability to make things too.

Father God, You are the Creator. Everything You have made is so amazing! Thank You for giving us the ability to think, work, and play. Help us use our skills for You. Amen.

THOUGHTS FOR DADDY

What's the most complicated thing you've ever created? Have you ever spent a weekend on a project that required multiple trips to a home-improvement store? Remarkably, God made everything out of nothing. He spoke, and it existed. God gave us the ability to *sub-create*, or to take what He has created and form it into works of art, machines, desserts, and more.

When God the Son became a human, He was a creator—a carpenter who made chairs and tables with His hands. Jesus dignified manual labor, demonstrating that everyone from a janitor to a brain surgeon can reflect God in her craft and make this world better. How do the different kinds of work you do glorify the Creator?

54

ALIKE AND DIFFERENT

He himself gave some to be apostles, some prophets, some evangelists, some pastors and teachers.
—Ephesians 4:11

What are two or three of your favorite things to do? Now think of your best friend. Does he like to do the exact same things as you? What does she like to do that's unlike you? Every person is *unique*, or different from others. People look different, like different things, and have different abilities. For example, some people like horses and riding bikes. Others like princesses and painting.

But did you know that all people have something important in common? God made everyone in His image! So even though we are all different, we are all alike in that way. Every person matters because every person, in his own way, can show us something about God. Isn't that amazing?

Father God, we can look around at our friends and neighbors, and we see how creative You are. Thank You for making us all alike and different. Amen.

THOUGHTS FOR DADDY

Think about the friends you spend the most time with. What do you have in common? Do your friends have any interests or preferences that you don't share? What do you learn from them because of that difference?

God created everyone in His image, but we each have our own distinctions. God gives people a wide range of talents, interests, and abilities, yet every single human has dignity and worth.

Have you ever considered how our differences can teach us about God? How does someone who's completely different from you reveal something about God's character? How does the diversity of believers in the church display God's beauty?

A CHURCH HOME

You are no longer foreigners and strangers,
but fellow citizens with the saints,
and members of God's household.
—Ephesians 2:19

Who are some of your friends at church? Do you remember your teacher's name? Church is a place to meet together to worship God. We pray, sing songs, read the Bible, and learn about Jesus with other people who love Him. The church is where all different kinds of people who believe in God come together.

Did you know the Bible says that the church is like a family (Ephesians 1:5)? We love one another, take care of one another, and need one another. We remind each other that God is great and He loves us. What do you like the most about going to church?

Father God, thank You for the church.
The church is like our family on earth while
we wait for Jesus to come back. Meet with us
as we worship You as a church. Amen.

THOUGHTS FOR DADDY

Think about the church where you worship. Why do you participate in the church? What role has the church served in your growth? Why do you think God wants believers to meet together as the church?

The church is God's good idea. It is a home for His children on earth. In the church, believers find encouragement, restoration, and exhortation. The church is also God's instrument for spreading the gospel to all nations.

It's important to remember that the church is not a man-made institution. It's the beautiful bride of Christ (Revelation 19:7). Jesus loves the church. He builds it up as He saves sinners, and the church is a forever home for believers.

56

WHY CHURCH?

*Until I [Paul] come, give your attention
to public reading, exhortation, and teaching.*
—1 Timothy 4:13

Where do we go if we need to buy groceries? We go to the grocery store! Where do we go to get some books to read? We go to the library or the bookstore! Where do we go to learn about God? We go to church!

The *church* is people who follow Jesus meeting together to listen to God's Word, worship Him, and serve others. Church leaders, like a pastor, teach from the Bible to help us learn about God. We worship God by singing songs, praying, giving money, and more. We serve others by praying for them or helping them when they're in need.

What have you learned about God at church? What's your favorite way to worship God?

Father God, thank You for the church!
We ask that You give our church leaders
everything they need as they lead us.
Help us love and serve the church. Amen.

THOUGHTS FOR DADDY

How would you describe your commitment to the church right now? Can you grow and mature as a Christian without gathering with the body of Christ?

Read Hebrews 10:24–25. The church matters to God. Believers all around the world meet regularly as smaller congregations to sing praises, worship, hear the Bible proclaimed, be baptized, share the Lord's Supper, serve one another, hold one another accountable, and urge one another to love and good deeds. These are all practices that are either difficult or impossible to do on our own. As you gather with your church, consider the role God has for you there. How you can bless and encourage others as you follow Jesus?

57
OUR CHURCH FAMILY

Think about the people in our family. Is everyone good at doing the same things, or do we divide up the work? Is someone the best at cooking? Who cares for the pets most? Does someone want to do the yardwork? As a family, we live, work, and play together every day. Everyone has an important role in our family!

The church is God's family. As part of the church, everyone has a place and work they can do to help—even kids! The church works together to serve God. What is something you are good at? How could you use your skills to help out at church?

Father God, You created the church to be a family. You give everyone special skills so the church can be taken care of. Help us know how to love the people in our church family. Amen.

THOUGHTS FOR DADDY

Think about your family. At home, what expectations do you have for family members about helping out? How do you expect your children to treat their brothers and sisters? Even if they don't like each other sometimes, you expect them to love one another and learn about what that love looks like.

God designed the church to be like a family, and for believers to be brothers and sisters in Christ (Matthew 12:48–50). We "rejoice with those who rejoice; weep with those who weep" (Romans 12:15). We meet needs, pray, and encourage one another to keep on following Jesus. Through open and honest conversations, we help one another resist temptation. When Jesus is our greatest treasure, we have unity within the family of God.

58

ON A MISSION

"Go, therefore, and make disciples of all nations, baptizing them in the name of the Father and of the Son and of the Holy Spirit."
—Matthew 28:19

Has anyone ever given you a job to do at home? Maybe you got to set the table, water the plants, or put away some of the groceries. Those jobs don't take long, and some of them you can even do by yourself.

Did you know that God gives the church a job to do? It's a special mission that all believers work together to accomplish: we are to tell others about Jesus! God wants everyone to know about Jesus and how He rescues people from their sins. We can tell our family members, our friends, our neighbors, and everyone about Jesus!

Who do you want to tell about Jesus? What might you say?

*Father God, thank You for Jesus! He saves us
from our sins, and that is good news!
Help us carry out Your mission for the church
by telling everyone we meet about Him. Amen.*

THOUGHTS FOR DADDY

What do you most want to accomplish in life? How do you want to be remembered after you die?

If you are a believer, God calls you to look beyond the accolades the world offers. He invites you into something way more exciting: the Great Commission. "Go . . . and make disciples of all nations," Jesus said, and He guarantees our success in fulfilling this mission.

Read Matthew 16:18. Jesus promises to build His church. Your role in making disciples may be unique and exciting, or it might look ordinary or simple. But everyone in the church has the privilege of sharing the good news with the world. Does Jesus' mission for the church excite you? Why or why not?

59

HAPPY HELPERS

"It is more blessed to give
than to receive."
—Acts 20:35

Can you think of a time you needed help? It's okay to ask for help when you need it! Can you think of a time you helped someone else? It feels good to be a helper, doesn't it?

When Jesus was on earth, He helped a lot of people, but He didn't go to the people who thought they could do everything on their own; He went to the people who truly needed help.

God wants the people in His church to be helpers like Jesus, to take care of people in their community who don't have anyone else to take care of them. We can pray for people, share meals and gifts with them, listen to them, and more. How can you be a helper?

*Father God, You sent the biggest help ever!
You gave us Jesus to help us and rescue
us from our sins. Help us work together as
the church to help others. Amen.*

THOUGHTS FOR DADDY

As the daddy of a preschooler, how many times a day do you stop what you are doing to help tie a shoe or prepare a snack? At what point do you start feeling weary of your child's neediness?

As adults, we might try to act like we are fine on our own, but we are needy creatures too. Are you afraid that God might get sick of you if you came to Him for help as often as you truly need it? Think again. Consider the type of people Jesus was drawn to on earth—the orphans, the widows, the blind, the uneducated, the outcasts. God is drawn to the vulnerable, to the ones who admit that they cannot do life without Him.

60

HE'S THE BOSS

He is also the head of the body, the church; he is
the beginning, the firstborn from the dead, so that
he might come to have first place in everything.
—*Colossians 1:18*

Who is in charge at home? Your parents! God gave
you parents who love you and take care of you.

Remember, the church is like a family. Do you
know who is in charge of the church? You might
think pastors or the preachers. They are leaders of
the church, but Jesus is the One truly in charge of
God's church. He's the boss of everyone else! We can
serve Jesus with joy because He is good. When we
follow Jesus, we decide that we are not in charge
of our own lives. Instead, we let Him be the boss and
we follow Him.

Father God, You gave us Jesus as the head of the church. Help us remember that our hope is not in human leaders but in Jesus, who loves us and takes care of us. Amen.

THOUGHTS FOR DADDY

Have you ever had a boss at work who was great? How about less than great? What was the difference between them?

The Bible says that the church is like a body, and Jesus is the head (Colossians 1:18). Jesus is also the Good Shepherd, and we are His sheep (John 10:3–4, 11). The church is His bride, and He is the bridegroom (Revelation 19:7). Which of these images resonates with you most? Which is hardest for you to picture? Combine all these images, and we know that Jesus is a loving and good boss. We can follow Him joyfully all our lives.

The Lord will fulfill his purpose for me. Lord,
your faithful love endures forever; do not
abandon the work of your hands.
—Psalm 138:8

GOD'S PURPOSES

Purpose is a big word. Do you know what it means? What's the purpose of a knife, bed, toothbrush, schoolbook, or airplane? When something has a purpose, that means there is a reason we use it. If the thing breaks, we try to fix it so that we can use it again.

All humans were made for one main purpose: to *glorify*, or honor, God. This means, with God's love in our hearts, we walk around with gladness, serving Him and others. The problem is, all of our hearts are broken. We cannot fulfill our purpose well because of our sin. We walk around worried, angry, and selfish. But there is good news! Jesus came to earth to remind us of God's main purpose for us. Jesus died for our sins so our broken hearts could be healed and we could glorify God again. In this section, we will learn all about God's good purposes for us.

MADE WITH PURPOSE

I call to God Most High, to God
who fulfills his purpose for me.
—Psalm 57:2

When something has *purpose* that means there is a reason we use it. For example, what is the purpose of a book? To read. What is the purpose of a crayon? To color. What is the purpose of a fork? To eat with.

The Bible says that you have a purpose! This means you have a reason for being on earth, and there is a reason God made you how He did. First of all, God wants you to know Jesus and trust in Him. Second of all, God gave you special skills and abilities to show others God's love and help them see what Jesus is like. That sounds like a pretty important purpose, doesn't it?

Father God, You created us with a special purpose. Help us live in a way that honors You. We want to please You with our lives. Amen.

THOUGHTS FOR DADDY

Have you ever spent much time thinking about why you are on earth? God made people with a purpose. God didn't create us to pursue wealth, fame, and our own happiness. He wants us to be happy, but He has *eternity* in mind.

God created you to know Him and find your joy in Him. Before you were born, God knew what you'd be like, and He has a plan to glorify Himself through you. This means your life matters. The place you live, the job you work, your marital status, and who you know are all part of God's plan for you. Do you hold tight to your own plans for your life, or are you open to God's leading?

NUMBER THE DAYS

Your eyes saw me when I was formless;
all my days were written in your book
and planned before a single one of them began.
—*Psalm 139:16*

How old are you? How old will you be on your next birthday? Do you know how old I am? How old will I be on my next birthday?

Every day that God gives us in this life is a gift. The Bible says that people don't know how long they will live before they die, but God knows. God may bless us with many years on earth, or He may give us a shorter life. Instead of worrying about how long or short our life will be, we can trust in God's plan for us and live every day on purpose—learning to serve God and love Him as the greatest treasure we could ever have.

Father God, thank You for today. Help us remember that You made us and give us life every day. We want each day to count for You. Amen.

THOUGHTS FOR DADDY

As we experience the monotony of our daily routine, it can be difficult to appreciate our life as well as difficult to remember that one day, our life on earth will end.

God knows the exact number of days you will live. You may live forty or sixty or eighty years, so *how* should you live? Read Psalm 90:12. The Bible calls us to be wise with the time we have. Take risks for Jesus. Make your life count for eternity. The best way we can spend our lives is in service to God, who has rescued us from sin and death. We can make each day count when we walk with God in love and obedience.

LOVE AND OBEY

If you could do anything you want tomorrow, what would you do? Now think about when you grow up. What do you want to do then?

God has given you so much; you could do so many things! As you grow and discover what you like and what you are good at, remember this: God made you and He loves you. He can use you in His great, big plan to tell the whole world about Jesus. Whether you are a teacher, parent, artist, doctor, or anything else, the most important thing you can do is love God and obey Him. Life works best when we live it for God.

Father God, help us remember that You created us to love You and obey You. Show us that life works best when we live it for You. Amen.

THOUGHTS FOR DADDY

Do you think God cares about your job? How about who you marry or how many kids you have? How about how you spend your free time?

God cares about all the details of our lives, but those decisions are not the *most* important decisions we will make. More than anything else, God wants us to love Him and obey Him wherever we are. Following Jesus is a daily commitment, no matter what our circumstances might be. The more love and obedience remain our focus, the more joy we find. When we live this way, the details of our lives may not be our final aim, but they become full of meaning. Life really does work best when our focus stays on God.

DOING GOOD WORKS

We are his workmanship, created in Christ Jesus for good
works, which God prepared ahead of time for us to do.
—Ephesians 2:10

Sometimes I ask you to do things around the house.
What are some of those things? Maybe you carry
your plate to the sink when you are done eating, or
you pick up your toys in your room.

Now, when I ask you to do something for me, is it
because I want you to earn my love? No way! I would
still love you even if you never did those things. But
perhaps you do them because you already know I
love you, and you love me too.

God dòes not ask us to do good things to earn
His love. He already loves us! But God is happy when
we do what He asks because of our love for Him.

Father God, You gave us good works to do. Help us remember that we don't have to do good works to earn Your love. You already love us so much! Amen.

THOUGHTS FOR DADDY

Many world religions hold to the belief that a person is saved from his sins by doing good works. People must do more good things than bad in life to be accepted by God. Christianity, on the other hand, teaches that we can never save ourselves. Salvation comes only through trusting in Jesus and His finished work on the cross.

So if we are not saved by good works, why is doing good works important for our faith? Because goodness is a reflection of God's character (Psalm 119:68), and God has purposed good works for each of us (Ephesians 2:10). Once we have experienced God's goodness, we don't do good because we *have* to; we do good because we *want* to.

NOT ALWAYS EASY

Have I ever asked you to do something hard? For example, if you make a huge mess in your room, and I tell you to pick up your toys, that might sound hard. Cleaning your room is a big job. But if it's way too big, I can help you make it clean and safe again.

Sometimes God asks us to do things that are not easy. This is one of His purposes for Christians. For example, forgiving people who hurt us can be hard, but He says to do it. Loving brothers and sisters can be hard, but He says to do that too. What if God asks something too big for us? That's okay—He will help!

Father God, sometimes You ask us to do hard things. Help us remember that we can do hard things because You will help us. Amen.

THOUGHTS FOR DADDY

Is the Christian life supposed to be easy? Read Acts 14:22. The Bible says that enduring many hardships is necessary to enter God's kingdom.

Living for Jesus will be hard, but He is worth every moment. Jesus takes us against the ways of the world. Let's not give our children an unrealistic picture of being a Christian. Jesus' kingdom is an upside-down kingdom, meaning that as we lay down our lives, we find true life. Are you living in an upside-down kingdom right now, or are you living to optimize your own comfort, security, and self-preservation? Look to the life of Jesus and follow His example.

WHAT'S THE PLAN?

A person's heart plans his way,
but the Lord determines his steps.
—Proverbs 16:9

Can you think of a time you made a plan to do something, like go to the library or the zoo? Often when we make plans, it works out. Other times, it doesn't. Like maybe the library is closed for cleaning, or the zoo is closed because of bad weather. Our plans might have to change because things happen that are out of our control.

Do you know that God is always in control? Whatever God plans, it happens. He is never surprised by a sudden rain shower or frustrated by a locked door. We can trust God with our plans because He is in control, and He always does what is best.

Father God, You are in control of all things.
You have a plan for us, and it is always good.
Help us trust You. Amen.

THOUGHTS FOR DADDY

Think about a time you made plans and they didn't pan out. If you had anything planned in 2020 beyond the month of February, it was likely canceled—or at least subject to different guidelines. Things like global pandemics may surprise us, but God was not surprised by COVID-19. We make plans, but God decides what happens.

Read Proverbs 16:9. Do you trust God's control over all things? Are you ever tempted to think your plans are greater than His? On the flip side, are you tempted to never make plans because they probably won't happen anyway? Trust that God's sovereignty and our free will both exist, and then make proactive decisions in faith accordingly.

FOR OUR GOOD

We know that all things work together for
the good of those who love God,
who are called according to his purpose.
—Romans 8:28

Do you like puzzles? Puzzles can be hard, especially if they have a lot of pieces! Puzzles with one hundred or five hundred pieces can take a long time to put together. When you see only one small piece at a time, it's hard to figure out what the big picture is.

Sometimes life is like that. Good things and bad things happen, and it can be hard to know why they are happening because we don't see the big picture. Do you know who *does* see it? God sees! He is in control of everything, and He uses even the bad things to bring about good. God's purposes will always be for good in the end.

Father God, You are so big! Sometimes things happen that seem so wrong, but we know we are small. We do not see the big picture. Help us trust You to work out all things for our good. Amen.

THOUGHTS FOR DADDY

Think of the last time your child went to the doctor. If he received vaccinations or blood work, how did he handle the shot? Children cry because shots hurt, but we don't withhold them for that reason. We comfort them through the experience, knowing the momentary pain, which we too have experienced, is for their benefit.

We might often wonder how a good God can allow His children to hurt. But when that's the case, we can remember our God does not stand far off. Jesus is the incarnate God; He understands suffering and offers salvation through suffering, for by His wounds we are healed (Isaiah 53:5). Jesus is working all evil, suffering, and pain out for our good.

ALWAYS ON PURPOSE

Everything was created by him,
in heaven and on earth . . . all things have
been created through him and for him.
—Colossians 1:16

Have you ever made a craft for someone to use? What did you make? What was it for? Things that people make usually have a purpose. Chairs are for sitting. Vases are for holding flowers. Soap is for washing our hands.

Have you ever wondered why God made the world? God made the whole world for a reason: to show His *glory*. That means everything in the world—even what happens or does not happen—is to show *how great God is*. God has a purpose for where we live, who our neighbors are, and who's in our family. Our purpose as humans is also to show God's glory, wherever we are.

Father God, even the birds chirp and the cats purr to show Your glory. Help us glorify You too. You are amazing, and we praise You! Amen.

THOUGHTS FOR DADDY

Have you ever looked around and felt like the world was completely out of control? From global turmoil to the chaos in our own homes, it is clear that we have little power to make things happen just how we want. On the flip side, have you recently enjoyed a moment of stillness or silence? A moment when you could hear God speaking to you through all the chaos in His still, small voice?

God stands behind both the chaos and the calm. The same powerful God who sent plagues into Egypt and quieted the stormy seas rules today. He is at work, and in the end, there is purpose in everything He's doing: to bring Himself glory and bring good for His people.

A PIECE OF THE PUZZLE

In the same way we who are many are one body in Christ and individually members of one another.
—Romans 12:5

How many fingers do you have? How many ears? How many arms? Each part of your body is important and does something different. Could you try to taste food with your fingers? Would your arms be very good at listening? No, that's silly! God made your body, and each part of your body has a different purpose.

In a similar way, God has a purpose for every person who's part of His church. Some people teach, some people welcome others, some clean up, and others lead worship. Everyone works together in different ways, like parts of a body. God has a place in the church for you too!

Father God, You have a special role for each of us in Your church. Help us work together to serve You and tell the whole world about Jesus. Amen.

THOUGHTS FOR DADDY

The church is an essential part of God's purpose for the world. It works like a body to remind us that we are a part of something bigger than ourselves. The church is all about Jesus! Believers in the church possess God-given gifts to help us carry out God's plan to make disciples of Jesus.

What has God gifted you to do? Read Ephesians 4:11. The diversity of gifts among believers shows the beauty of God's plan for the church. God has purposed for us to honor one another's strengths and embrace our own, whether in evangelism, pastoring, serving, giving, administration, teaching, encouraging, or whatever you're gifted to do.

70

BE HOLY

You planned evil against me; God planned it
for good to bring about the present result—
the survival of many people.
—*Genesis 50:20*

Even though most of us want to make good choices, it's very hard for us to do so. In the Bible, there's a story of some brothers who sold one of their brothers into slavery because they were jealous of him. Years later, their brother (who had been a slave) had become second in command to the king! When the brothers came to his land looking for help, they couldn't believe it. God had taken their wrong choice and turned it into something good. Their brother forgave them, and their family was saved.

Stories like this one remind us to trust God in everything. Even when people make wrong choices (and when we do too), God is always up to something good.

Father God, thank You for loving us. You see and know everything. When You allow bad things to happen, You have a good reason. Help us trust You to take care of us. Amen.

THOUGHTS FOR DADDY

These are big thoughts for little hearts, but there's no better time than now to introduce kids to the God who sits on the throne. He is so strong; He could stop bad things from happening. Many people conclude that because the world is so bad, God must not be good.

But the Bible is full of stories of God allowing evil to happen and then, in the end, always accomplishing the good He intends. We may not understand some of the horrible things He allows, but we can trust that the Lord understands things we cannot because He is God. Meditate on the good that comes from the cross, and trust that no evil can stop God from fulfilling His purposes in this world.

Instruct the wise, and he will be wiser still; teach the righteous, and he will learn more. "The fear of the LORD is the beginning of wisdom, and the knowledge of the Holy One is understanding."
—*Proverbs 9:9–10*

WISDOM

What is something you're learning about right now? Is it animals? Numbers? Letters? Music? God has filled this world with so many things to learn about! The older you get, the more knowledge your brain will hold. But sometimes when people learn a lot of things, they start to think that they have all the answers. Sometimes you even think you know better than Mommy or Daddy, don't you?

People who are wise understand that God is the only One who knows everything and that we all need His help to get through life. The wise person might be smart, but she doesn't think she is smarter than other people, and she definitely doesn't believe she is smarter than God. The wise person listens to God and lets Him lead every part of life. In this section, we'll learn more about how to be wise people.

WHERE IS WISDOM?

My dear brothers and sisters,
understand this: Everyone should be quick
to listen, slow to speak, and slow to anger.
—James 1:19

Can you point to your nose? You use your nose to smell things! Now point to your ears. What are your ears for? Listening! Can you point to your brain? You use your brain for thinking, and it helps you make choices.

The Bible says there is a special ability that helps us make right choices. It's called *wisdom*. We can get wisdom by living according to God's words in the Bible. Foolishness is the opposite of wisdom. The foolish person believes he is better than others; the wise person understands he has flaws. The foolish person talks quickly without listening; the wise person thinks before she speaks. God gives us wisdom; all we have to do is ask!

Father God, all wisdom comes from You. Help us listen to what You say and do what You say. Please give us wisdom and help us make right choices to honor You. Amen.

THOUGHTS FOR DADDY

Having wisdom helps us know what to do. Wisdom helps us understand the world around us. Where do you search for wisdom? True wisdom comes from God alone. He created everything and knows how life works best.

Read James 1:5. We can get wisdom by asking God for it. We can study His Word and then do what it says. The more we do this, the more God's way of living proves itself to be best. Wisdom is not merely suggestions for living; it is part of God's plan for our sanctification. Wisdom in the Bible shows us how to be like Jesus—in how we live, how we speak, and how we think. What decision do you need wisdom to make?

THE POWER TO DO RIGHT

Keep the LORD's commands and statutes
I am giving you today, for your own good.
—Deuteronomy 10:13

If I gave you a cookie and then told you not to eat it yet, could you wait? If I left the room, would it be harder not to take a bite?

Sometimes we know the right thing to do, but it feels so hard to do. God made us, and He has told us what is right. God tells us in the Bible how He wants us to live. Sometimes following God's rules can be very hard, but God wants us to do what He says because His rules are good for us. God also helps us obey Him. When we pray, He gives us power to do what is right.

Father God, help us remember that Your rules are good. You want what is best for us. Give us power to obey because we love You. Amen.

THOUGHTS FOR DADDY

Do God's commands ever feel too difficult (or even unnecessary) to obey? One way the Holy Spirit empowers us to obey God is by helping us trust God's promises.

God will meet your deepest desires in His perfect timing. The more we obey, the happier we actually become. God's promises are full of everything we could ever desire in relationship to Jesus. Sin is getting what we want in our time and in our own way. Disobedience will never leave you satisfied in the long run. Ask the Lord for strength to obey, and trust that all God's promises will come true in Christ at the right time.

73

DEALING WITH ANGER

Be angry and do not sin.
Don't let the sun go down on your anger.
—Ephesians 4:26

Think of a time when you felt angry. Maybe someone took a toy from you, or maybe Daddy said no to you. What did you do? When you feel angry, you might notice your heart beating faster or your ears getting warm. You might want to yell or hit or scream! But what is the right thing to do?

In the Bible, God tells us what to do when we feel angry. God tells us to be slow to anger (James 1:19). It tells us to be careful not to sin when we feel angry. We can close our eyes, take deep breaths, and pray when we feel angry. God created you with all of your emotions, and He helps you know what to do with them.

Father God, sometimes we feel angry.
Keep us from sinning when we feel angry.
Help us slow down and control our
emotions in a way that honors You. Amen.

THOUGHTS FOR DADDY

What do you think about anger? Is God okay with us feeling angry? Read Ephesians 4:26. "Be angry" is a command, with "do not sin" as the guardrail. Jesus, who never sinned, felt angry. He overturned tables in the temple because people were treating it like a marketplace (Matthew 21:12). Not all anger leads to sin. There is a righteous anger that is against the things God hates.

But the Bible urges us to be slow to anger. When you feel anger stirring up inside you, take a deep breath. Pray. Ask God if this anger comes from a place of sin or of righteousness. Fight against sinful anger that glorifies yourself, and seek the glory of God.

74

HUMBLE RUMBLE

He gives greater grace. Therefore he says: God resists the proud but gives grace to the humble.
—James 4:6

Who is the most important? Is it a movie star? Is it a president or prince? Is it you? People are not the most important; God is! Sometimes we forget that. We want the biggest piece of cake or we don't want to share our toys because we think we are the most important.

Pride is thinking that you are the best or the most important. Pride is wrong because it's not true. The opposite of pride is *humility*. Humility is understanding that God is most important and that you are not better than other people. We must be humble to see that we are sinners who need God to help and forgive us. Let's ask God to take away our pride.

Father God, You are wise and good. We are sometimes prideful, but we want to be humble. Help us be like Jesus and consider others more important than ourselves. Amen.

THOUGHTS FOR DADDY

While the world puts value on achievements—top-ten lists, halls of fame, world records—the kingdom of God values humility. Humility comes when we recognize the truth about God and about ourselves. The fact is, we aren't the greatest. God is. Coming to Jesus as a needy sinner requires humility. We have to admit that we don't have it all together.

God gives us skills and talents not to point people to us and how great we are, but to point people to Him and His greatness! Read Psalm 115:1. Spend time in prayer, confessing areas where you are tempted to be proud. Ask God to give you a spirit like Christ—a spirit of humility.

TELL THE TRUTH

Lying lips are detestable to the Lord,
but faithful people are his delight.
—*Proverbs 12:22*

Did you know Daddy has told a lie before? I could tell you stories of when I lied and how I got caught. It is always embarrassing.

Telling the truth is hard, but it is always the right thing to do. God always tells us the truth. In fact, He *is* the Truth. The Bible says there is someone who always lies: Satan. He hates God and he hates us, so he tries to trick us into thinking lying is no big deal.

We might feel afraid to tell the truth because the truth might be embarrassing. But when we tell the truth about our sin—when we are *honest*—we can be made right with God and each other.

Father God, You delight in the truth, and You are the Truth. Help us tell the truth even when it is hard. Amen.

THOUGHTS FOR DADDY

Read 1 John 1:7. Telling the truth is like walking in the light. Lying is like being in the dark. As Christians, we live our lives in the light, where Jesus is. This means we are known as we truly are. We can tell the truth about ourselves and what we've done. Instead of being met with judgment, we are met by the Friend of sinners—Jesus—with His own blood ready to cleanse us from all sin! Living in the light leads us to true friendship with God and with one another.

What do you need to be honest about before God and others? What part of your life have you kept in the dark and need to bring into the light?

YES AND NO

As you get older, I need to be able to trust you. Not only me, but God wants you to grow into a trustworthy person too. To be *trustworthy* means when we say we will do something, we do it! This is not always easy, but it is the wise thing to do. Fools break their word, but wise people keep it.

Do you know why this is so important? Well, when we are trustworthy, people can rely on us. This shows what God is like. Jesus asks us to be trustworthy because He Himself is the most trustworthy of all. Jesus means what He says and will do what He says.

Father God, thank You for being trustworthy.
Help us mean what we say and do it. Help us
keep our word and honor You. Amen.

THOUGHTS FOR DADDY

Who is the most trustworthy person you know? Do you consider yourself to be trustworthy? Are you trustworthy in certain circumstances more than others?

How amazing is it that God has made commitments to us and has sworn by Himself to keep them (Genesis 22:16)? Jesus is the greatest fulfillment of God's commitment to save His people. Fulfilling our commitments is important—even when it's frustrating, annoying, or seemingly unnecessary—because we tell the world what God is like when we are trustworthy. When we mess up and don't follow through on our word, we still have a Savior in Jesus, who forgives. Praise God for the trustworthiness of our Lord Jesus!

HARD AT WORK

Whatever you do, do it from the heart,
as something done for the Lord and not for people.
—*Colossians 3:23*

I love it when you succeed. When you catch a pass, hit a ball, or win a game, I clap and cheer! When you sing a song, play an instrument, draw a picture, or build a fort, it makes me happy.

Did you know that God does the same thing? He rejoices over you when you work with all your heart to do something. God always sees you when you are learning new things. He never misses a ball game or a dance recital. He even sees you when you are all alone. God wants you to work hard at everything you do—this is a wise choice! So we do our best and then relax about it, remembering that God loves us no matter what.

Father God, thank You for creating us to be
makers and doers in Your world. You see everything
we work hard at and take delight in it. Amen.

THOUGHTS FOR DADDY

As you coach or watch your kids work hard at something, keep in perspective what will matter in ten, twenty, and fifty years. Godly character, wisdom, and work ethic will matter more than the mastery of any activity. Character is built by working for the Lord, who is always with us.

As you model a wise work ethic for your kids, remember that the Lord is completely for us. He is not standing over our shoulders with a disapproving scowl. No matter what type of boss you have, you can work hard in the security of God's full acceptance through Jesus. Work hard not to earn the recognition or approval of men, but knowing you already have the full approval of the God of the universe.

BEING A FRIEND

"Just as you want others to do for you,
do the same for them."
—Luke 6:31

Who is your best friend? How does your friend treat you? Sometimes our friends might hurt us or disappoint us. What is the wise way to treat our friends?

Jesus tells us to love people just how we want to be loved. We can imagine how we would want our friends and neighbors to interact with us and then go do just that for them. For example, do you ever wish someone would go out of his way to play with you? Maybe you could do that for someone else who needs a new friend. Jesus says the wisest way to be a friend and neighbor is to do for others what we'd want them to do for us.

*Father God, thank You for loving us
even when we didn't love You. Help us do
for others what You have done for us—
You loved us and served us first. Amen.*

THOUGHTS FOR DADDY

Read Matthew 7:12. The golden rule may be one of Jesus' most well-known and celebrated commands. What would it look like to live this out with your family? How can your family members be proactive in loving one another and loving your neighbors?

Imagine the ideal neighbor, father, or husband. Are you like that? None of us is perfect, but Jesus empowers us to love and serve those around us without hesitating or expecting something in return. We are free to love like this because Jesus first loved us. He has given us everything we need for life and godliness (2 Peter 1:3).

WAITING IS HARD TO DO

If we hope for what we do not see,
we eagerly wait for it with patience.
—Romans 8:25

Is waiting hard for you too? What is something you're really looking forward to right now? We can get cranky and demanding when we don't get *what* we want *when* we want it. Sometimes we even throw tantrums or shout at others because we hate waiting so much.

In this life, there are many things we have to wait for. We wait for God to answer our prayers. We wait to see what the future holds. Most important of all, we are waiting for Jesus to come back to earth! Wise people understand that waiting is a part of being human, and they wait patiently. While we wait, God will give us what we need to trust in Him.

Father God, give us patience while we wait for the things we want and need. Help us trust You. And thank You that Jesus is coming back! We wait eagerly for Him. Amen.

THOUGHTS FOR DADDY

Scripture makes it clear that the wise are patient (Proverbs 19:11) and wait on the Lord (Psalm 130:5). Faith itself is an act of waiting. We walk now by faith in Jesus, believing that one day all of His promises will come to pass. One day it will not be strange to believe Jesus is the Son of God because He will return in glory, and every knee will bow and every tongue will confess that He is Lord (Philippians 2:10–11).

How will you live while you wait? Our time of patiently waiting isn't a season of inactivity but of faithfully following Jesus day by day. Waiting is hard, but God's timing is always perfect.

SHARING MADE SIMPLE

A generous person will be blessed,
for he shares his food with the poor.
—Proverbs 22:9

Would you rather get a present or give someone else a present? Jesus teaches us that it is better to give than to receive (Acts 20:35). Do you feel good when you share your toys or favorite treats? The more we practice sharing and giving, the easier it will be to give things away to people who need them.

Wise people understand that we are *generous*, or happy to give, because God is generous with us. People are more important than toys or treats. Remember that everything we own comes from God, and He has given us things to help those around us. Who is someone you want to be generous with this week?

Father God, all we have is Yours.
Help us be generous and share with others.
Remind us that You shared generously
with us when You gave us Jesus. Amen.

THOUGHTS FOR DADDY

Are you generous? Generosity is a response to grace, and it is an act of worship and love. We can force ourselves to give, but we can't fake generosity. When we truly understand what Christ gave up so that we could be brought into God's family, we are free and eager to give ourselves away.

Remember, generosity is more than about giving away money. You can give of your time, talents, and other resources. Throughout the Bible, there is a prominent theme of God blessing His people not because they deserve it, but *so that* they could become a blessing to others. If you struggle with being generous, consider what you might wrongly believe about God or yourself.

A friend loves at all times, and a brother
is born for a difficult time.
—Proverbs 17:17

FAMILY AND FRIENDS

Family and friends are two of the most important things God has given us. God made family members to help us grow, learn about the world, and care for one another. There's a story in the Bible about a mother, Naomi, and her daughter-in-law, Ruth. Ruth said to Naomi, "Wherever you go, I will go, and wherever you live, I will live; your people will be my people, and your God will be my God" (Ruth 1:16). This was a powerful commitment to a family member.

The Bible also describes a special friendship: "Jonathan was bound to David in close friendship, and loved him as much as he loved himself" (1 Samuel 18:1). This is how God asks us to love one another: as we love ourselves. In this section, we'll see how to be godly family members and friends.

IN THIS TOGETHER

Start a youth out on his way; even when he
grows old he will not depart from it.
—Proverbs 22:6

Jesus has called our whole family on an adventure together. This means you're included too! This adventure is following Jesus with our lives. We want to believe in Jesus and all that He has for us. We want to live like Jesus lived so that we honor Him and show everyone we know how much He has changed us. This is why we talk to Him by praying, and we listen to His words by reading the Bible together.

When we follow Jesus, He will lead us to love people who are not like us and to share with them the good news about God. This will be a great adventure, and Jesus will be with our family as we follow Him together!

Father God, thank You for our family.
We want to follow Jesus together.
Help us love one another as we do. Amen.

THOUGHTS FOR DADDY

Psalm 127:4–5 compares children to the arrows in the hand of a mighty man: "Happy is the man who has filled his quiver with them." Whether you have one child or many, God has given you an important role in your child's spiritual development.

As parents, we are like signs pointing our children somewhere. They are studying us, so we have the joyous privilege of being God's instrument to point them to the One who can save them. Thankfully, God will work through us in spite of our shortcomings. As we treasure Jesus and walk with Him, our children will witness God's faithfulness on display and hopefully follow Him too.

LISTEN, MY CHILDREN

Repeat [God's words] to your children. Talk about them when you sit in your house and when you walk along the road, when you lie down and when you get up.
—Deuteronomy 6:7

What days of the week can you read the Bible? Sunday, Monday, Tuesday, Wednesday, Thursday, Friday, or Saturday. Any day! We always read the Bible at church, but there is never a bad time to read God's Word or talk about Jesus. The more times we can find to think about God, the better. We are Christians at church, but we are also Christians wherever we are.

As your daddy, one of my jobs is to keep pointing you to God and His truth. This brings me joy because I know how much God loves us both, and my hope is that everyone in our family would love Him too!

Father God, thank You for the Bible and the truth that's inside it. Thank You for giving us a family to follow You together. Amen.

THOUGHTS FOR DADDY

Repetition is the key to spiritual formation. Humans are creatures of habit, and that's why God instructs us to talk about Jesus with our kids as often as we can. We can think of this as an ongoing conversation—one we put down and pick up again and again.

Also, if we aren't talking to our kids about the great news of the Bible, we can be sure that they will develop a worldview somewhere else. Shows, news, commercials, and friends are communicating different messages about what matters most in life. Let's form them in the good news of the gospel and wonderful ways of Jesus.

What has surprised you the most so far about talking to your child about Jesus?

83

O IS FOR OBEY

Children, obey your parents in everything,
for this pleases the Lord.
—Colossians 3:20

Sometimes obeying is hard, isn't it? I might ask you to do something you don't want to do. But learning to do what is right—even if it's not what you want to do—is important.

Why do you think obedience is so important? Why isn't it okay for you to just do whatever you want? Well, part of my job, as your daddy, is to help you understand how to live right. That's why God is happy when children obey their parents. God made you and gave you to me, but He also gave me to you to love and care for you. Isn't it a wonderful gift from God, that He gave us to each other?

Father God, You gave us parents who want what is best for us. Help us obey because it is right. We want to honor our parents and honor You. Amen.

THOUGHTS FOR DADDY

God loves us so much. He not only tells us what to do in His Word, but He also lets us in on the "why." The Bible is full of reasons to obey God. Sometimes sharing the "why" behind a command helps our children obey not just with their actions, but also with their hearts. One big "why" is that obedience pleases the Lord. If we love God, we do what He commands us.

As you instruct your child, reflect God's unconditional love. Obedience doesn't come naturally to anyone. When your child disobeys, use it as an opportunity to discipline in love. Remember, learning to submit to and obey parents is good practice for learning to submit to and obey the Lord.

84

KINDNESS MATTERS

How delightfully good when brothers
live together in harmony!
—Psalm 133:1

Think of when you play with other children. Do you like playing with kids when they are mean? I wouldn't either. But we all can be mean sometimes, can't we? Did you know that in heaven there will be no more fighting, name-calling, or making fun of others? That will be amazing!

Well, Jesus wants His followers to treat one another in this heavenly way now. We are kind to one another because God has been kind to us. God is slow to get angry, and He patiently waits for us to say sorry when we've done something wrong. With God's help, we can be kind to others.

Father God, thank You for sending Your Son, Jesus, who is gentle, understanding, and kind toward us. Help us be kind to others, especially if they are not kind to us. Amen.

THOUGHTS FOR DADDY

What words would you use to describe God? Do you think of Him as kind? We see God's kindness in His patience with us. Read Romans 2:4. God's patience and kindness are meant to lead us to repentance.

Have you ever thought about making kindness an expectation in your family? Sometimes it is easy to give a careless comment or harsh response to those we live with. Kindness at home can look like assuming the best of others, being quick to listen, and being patient with one another when we sin. We can cultivate kindness in our family that is a sweet foretaste of heaven. How will you model kindness at home?

85

WHAT IS A FRIEND?

"I give you a new command: Love one another. Just
as I have loved you, you are also to love one another."
—*John 13:34*

Can you imagine if there were no friends in the
world? That would be so sad because friends are
the best. Do you know the best way to find more
friends? Be a good friend! Friends listen and do
what's kind. They forgive one another. They help
each other and have fun together.

The Bible says that Jesus is the best Friend
anyone could have. Jesus' love is *sacrificial* love.
That means that He gave up something—His own
life by dying on the cross—so that we could be right
again with God. We can love our friends like Jesus
by doing good for them even when it is hard for us.

Father God, thank You for friends.
Help us be good friends by loving and
helping others. Most of all, thank You for
giving us the greatest Friend—Jesus! Amen.

THOUGHTS FOR DADDY

Who are your best friends? Probably those you can lean on in tough times. They do things like help you move, listen when you need to talk, and give you what you need before you even ask.

Sacrificial love is the greatest love. It can be boiled down to taking care of friends no matter what it takes. The costlier the love, the more like Jesus our love becomes. The greater the burden you carry, the deeper the love it is. God uses sacrificial love in redemptive ways because that type of love comes from His Spirit working inside us. How can you love your friends like Jesus?

86

LOVE YOUR ENEMIES

"I tell you, love your enemies and pray
for those who persecute you."
—Matthew 5:44

Have you ever heard the word *enemy*? An *enemy* describes a person who is mean to or hurts someone else. Has another kid ever tried to hurt you? What should you do when that happens? First, you tell an adult right away. After that, you can pray for that kid.

Does that surprise you? Why would we pray for people who are mean? Jesus teaches us that we should love our enemies. Jesus loved His enemies and even died on the cross for them, so He knows how hard this can be. But the Bible shows us that Jesus' love is powerful enough to turn His enemies into friends. If we love our enemies with the love of God, they just might become our friends too.

Father God, showing love to people who are mean to us is hard! Help us follow Jesus' example by loving our enemies with the love You put inside our hearts. Amen.

THOUGHTS FOR DADDY

Loving our enemies is counterintuitive. Getting even with people who have wronged us, holding it over their heads—these are the ways of the world. No other religion comes close to the redemptive love Jesus displays in dying for His enemies on the cross. Without this radical love, there would be no such thing as Christianity.

At the same time, loving our enemies does not include tolerating abuse. Jesus chose to love this way of His own volitation. People being abused have no power in the situation, while Jesus had all power and chose to give it up. We must shepherd our kids to be vigilant against abusive behaviors while also teaching the radical way of Jesus, who chose to die for His enemies.

87

LOVE YOUR NEIGHBOR

"Love your neighbor as yourself."
—Matthew 22:39

What is a neighbor? Who are the neighbors who live near us? Did you know that a neighbor can be anyone you meet? That's right—a *neighbor* is anyone God puts in your path!

The Bible says we should love our neighbors as ourselves. How much do you love yourself? You probably don't have a hard time making sure you eat, rest, and have fun. Loving ourselves comes naturally. So Jesus wants us to care about the people around us a lot! In fact, doing so is a part of God's greatest commandment. Think about how wonderful the world will be when we all truly love our neighbors.

Father God, thank You for giving us neighbors.
Help us love our neighbors as ourselves,
with the love that comes from You. Amen.

THOUGHTS FOR DADDY

The book of Luke records the story of a lawyer who wanted to excuse himself from Jesus' demands, so he asked Jesus, "Who is my neighbor?" (Luke 10:29). We do this all the time: keep a list of people we are responsible for and try not to extend ourselves too much beyond that.

Jesus challenges this position by encouraging us to love those who cross our path with the same love and attention we give ourselves. This sounds life-altering because it is. Jesus is turning our world upside down so that we love others with the same world-shaking love He showed by entering our world, hanging out with outcasts, and dying on a Roman cross. Who is the neighbor God is bringing to your mind right now?

88

WHO'S NUMBER ONE?

Everyone should look not to his own interests,
but rather to the interests of others.
—Philippians 2:4

When you play a board game with me or with friends, who wants to go first? Everyone says, "Me! Oh, I'll go first!" How would you feel if your friend said, "You can go first; I'll go last." That might sound strange because it seems better to be first, doesn't it?

The Bible teaches us that Jesus' way of living means putting others first. Jesus does not want us to just think about ourselves all the time. He wants us to put others' needs before our own. That means thinking about what people may want or need, even if it means giving up what you want or need. As Christians, we do this because that's what Jesus did for us.

Lord Jesus, thank You for not looking to Your own interests but to our interests. You came from heaven to earth to show us God's love. Help us show Your love to others. Amen.

THOUGHTS FOR DADDY

Jesus knew there was something to look forward to that would outweigh all He gave up when He came to earth. Read Hebrews 12:2. What was the joy set before Him as He endured the cross? Pleasing the Father who sent Him and saving all God's people through His sacrifice.

What will help us and our kids love and serve others even when it costs us a lot? Clinging to the joy that's set before us! That joy is pleasing God, and it helps others to know Christ and His great love. Do you put others first with this goal in mind or out of selfish motivations, to make them indebted to you? Consider how you might honor God in putting others first.

89

BEAR WITH ME

Walk worthy of the calling you have received,
with all humility and gentleness, with patience,
bearing with one another in love.
—Ephesians 4:1–2

If a friend or a sibling ruins something you love, what do you often do? Next time, try this: stop and think about it. Maybe your sister didn't mean to break your toy. Maybe your friend was in a hurry and lost control.

We all think we deserve to explode like a volcano when someone ruins what we love, but God wants us to be patient with others. "Bearing with one another" means learning to live with each other's mistakes without mistreating each other or lashing out. Remember, Jesus is patient with us. Let's give each other a break, forgive, and be gentle because we are all sinners who need God's grace.

Father God, You bear with us when we disobey You over and over. You do not turn away but draw us near to You. Help us be patient with others too. Amen.

THOUGHTS FOR DADDY

What are the marks of a Christian? How should a believer live? The Bible says our walk with Christ must be marked by humility, gentleness, and patience (Ephesians 4:1–2). Walking worthy of the calling we received is our chief aim as men who love Jesus. This means we live life in response to the gracious gift of sonship (1 John 3:1).

Paul's words do not call us to strive for anything, but to behave like the sons we already are. Do you have patience with your children? Do you bear your family's burdens? Do you hold your family's mistakes over them, or do you bear with them in love? Is your life marked by the patience of Christ?

90

HELLO, MY NAME IS . . .

This is good, and it pleases God our Savior,
who wants everyone to be saved and to come
to the knowledge of the truth.
—1 Timothy 2:3-4

Did you know that there are some people in the world who have never heard about God or His Son, Jesus? There are others who have never held or read a Bible. Isn't that sad?

God wants Christians to tell other people about Him! Whenever you'd like, you can tell your friends, neighbors, or family members anything you have learned about Jesus. You can share a Bible story or a song. God wants everyone to know Him. As you grow up, you will learn more about God, and I will help you! You can ask me questions and we will look for answers together. We can get to know God as a family.

Father God, You gave us a family to help us learn more about You. Give us chances to talk about You with our family, friends, and neighbors. Amen.

THOUGHTS FOR DADDY

Who first told you about Jesus? Maybe you grew up with believing parents, or maybe a friend invited you to church when you were a teenager. Every person has to decide in his life who he is going to live for. We can live for ourselves or we can live for God, who made us. Which do you choose?

Trusting in Jesus is the starting point for a lifelong mission of making disciples. God wants everyone to know Him. His heart is for people of every language, tribe, and nation. Begin with your kids. Tell them about Jesus. Help them grow in their awareness of their own sin, the lostness of the world, and the love and good news of Christ.

I will give you thanks with all my heart;
I will sing your praise before the heavenly
beings. I will bow down toward your hold temple
and give thanks to your name for your constant
love and truth. You have exalted your name and
your promise above everything else.
—*Psalm 138:1–2*

PRAYER AND PRAISE

When we have a personal relationship with God, everything in our life changes! Our hearts overflow with God's love in *prayer*, *worship*, *praise*, and *gratitude*. These are all big words that we will learn more about in this section, but they all reveal our love for God.

As Christians, we can't help but be excited about God. We talk to Him throughout our day. We share what He's doing in our lives—celebrating the good times and trusting in Him during the hard times. We thank Him for all the wonderful things He's given us. And we tell others that He loves them and wants to have a relationship with them too. A heart filled up with faith in God is a very full heart. Do you want to put your faith in God? Do you want Him to be in charge of your life?

WHAT IS PRAYER?

Listen, LORD, and answer me,
for I am poor and needy.
—Psalm 86:1

Do you know why we *pray*? When we pray, we aren't just talking to ourselves. We are talking to God, and He is listening! God loves when we talk to Him. You can tell Him what you liked about your day or what you are worried about. You can ask Him to heal people or help you get along with your siblings. You can tell Him how you are feeling or ask Him questions.

God answers our prayers in different ways. Sometimes He gives us an answer in our hearts. Other times, He works in the world. Sometimes God says yes or no, and other times, He says to wait. He often answers in ways we don't expect. Talk to God any time—He is happy to hear from you!

Father God, thank You for giving us a way to talk to You. Help us see the ways You answer our prayers and to trust that You are responding. Amen.

THOUGHTS FOR DADDY

God wants us to have a personal relationship with Him, which includes spending time in prayer. Think about the relationships in your home. You move about your day and speak frequently with each other. When you have friends over, you sit around the table and talk easily. By sharing your words, you are sharing your life.

God wants this kind of communication with us in prayer. Is this how you pray? Do you ask for what you need? Share your worries and concerns? Thank Him for what He's doing? Pause and listen for His still, small voice? The more time you spend in prayer, the more you realize your life belongs to God, and the more you build trust in Him.

HE'S ALL EARS

The righteous cry out, and the Lord hears,
and rescues them from all their troubles.
—Psalm 34:17

Have you ever tried to get my attention but I wasn't listening? Sometimes I am busy and don't hear you. You might have to tap me on the arm, speak louder, or wait patiently until I am ready to listen. When you talk to God, He always hears you. He is never too busy or too far away to listen. We can't see God, but He is near and hears us when we pray.

Prayer is powerful because God is powerful. He can hear every prayer from every heart around the world at the same time. God listens to our prayers and answers them in the best way.

Father God, right now You are listening to us. We don't have to pray special words or in a certain way to get Your attention. You hear us, and You answer. Thank You! Amen.

THOUGHTS FOR DADDY

Prayer is powerful because God hears our prayers. When we find ourselves in a tough situation, we ask our friends and family members to pray for us. We comfort others by offering prayer.

Prayer is not a lighthearted wish that things will turn out favorably; it is an appeal to the God of the universe. God listens to the prayers of His children and answers them. He listens to our confessions and forgives our sins. Do you pray with confidence that God hears? Do you pray with assurance that His answers are wise, even when you don't understand them? What have you been holding back from God that you need to pray about?

WHAT IS WORSHIP?

Is anyone among you suffering? He should pray.
Is anyone cheerful? He should sing praises.
—James 5:13

God tells us to sing to Him. Do you know why? God created people to worship Him. *Worship* is celebrating the greatness of God. It is how we show God that we love and respect Him.

But worship is more than just singing. Can you think of other ways we can show God that we love and respect Him? That's right! We can read the Bible and do what it says. We can pray. We can help and serve other people. We can dance, write, draw, build, teach, and use our different talents for God. All these things show God our love and respect for Him. What is your favorite way to worship and celebrate God?

Father God, You created us to worship You.
You are great! We want to celebrate who You are.
You are good and perfect. Amen.

THOUGHTS FOR DADDY

God created people to worship, and everyone is worshiping something. Some people worship other people. Some worship themselves. Some worship money. Others worship power. Some worship God.

God wants us to worship Him because only He deserves our worship. Dedicating your life to serving and worshiping God is never a futile endeavor. Read Romans 12:1. Christians worship God by choosing, every day, to go His way instead of our own. Worship is surrendering our hands, ears, mouths, and minds—our whole bodies—to the work and will of God. Is your life marked by worship of God or something else? What are you surrendered to?

94

OUR HEAVENLY FATHER

"Call to me and I will answer you and tell you great
and incomprehensible things you do not know."
—*Jeremiah 33:3*

Do you know that there is no wrong way to pray? Praying is as easy as talking to any person. God loves it when we pray. Do you know how I know? Because I love it when you come sit on my lap and talk to me.

God calls Himself our heavenly Father for a reason (Matthew 6:9). God has a soft spot in His heart for you—your stories, your dreams, and everything about you. What would you like to tell God? You can tell Him when you're happy, scared, or worried. You can ask Him for help and guidance. God loves it when we pray. Let's pray right now!

Father God, You are never bothered by our prayers. You love to hear us pray to You! We can pray any time about anything. Thank You for giving us the gift of prayer. Amen.

THOUGHTS FOR DADDY

Does the thought of praying make you feel energized or anxious? Like conversation, prayer can be learned and practiced. Since God is our heavenly Father, your prayers do not need to be long or eloquent. You can wake up and pray, "Lord, thanks for another day of life." You can pray as you get your child ready for the day. You can pray as you deal with her disobedience or bad attitudes.

Remember, God never grows tired of hearing from you. He is not annoyed with you. Be persistent with your prayers. Ask for what you need. Share how you feel. Go to the Father frequently because He wants to hear from you.

95

PRAYING FOR OTHERS

Confess your sins to one another and pray for one another, so that you may be healed. The prayer of a righteous person is very powerful in its effect.
—James 5:16

Have you ever helped someone else? Maybe a friend needed help moving a heavy toy or reaching a crayon. When someone has a problem, we can try to help. But what if we can't help? If someone is sick, can you heal him or her? No, but you can give comfort—maybe a pretty bouquet of flowers or a nice card.

The very best way we can help people is by praying for them. It might feel like praying isn't doing anything, but when you pray, you are asking the God of the universe for help. God can heal and comfort people. He can calm our hearts and minds. He can do miracles. Do you know anyone who needs our prayers today?

Father God, our friends, family members, and neighbors need Your help. We know some of them are hurting, sad, sick, or discouraged. We pray for them now and ask You to comfort them. Amen.

THOUGHTS FOR DADDY

Have you ever been struggling with something but no one else could help? Maybe anger, depression, or anxiety keeps you up at night. You could reach out to friends, but you think, *What could they do?*

Asking others to pray for you is a powerful and effective way to invite them to be with you through trials. You can pray for others too. Praying with others brings unity between believers. In fact, the Bible commands us to pray for one another. Prayer is a genuine way of caring for others. Whenever possible, follow up prayer with action. Read James 5:16. Do you need to ask others to pray for you about something? Who can you encourage through prayer?

96

WORTHY OF WORSHIP

Have you ever seen a rainbow? What did you do? You might have pointed to it and shouted, "A rainbow! Look!" Rainbows are pretty amazing, so when we see one, we react with excitement and want to tell others about it.

The Bible says that God is worthy of our *praise*. That means He deserves to be told how great He is. It's not that God wants to get compliments to feel good about Himself; God *is* perfectly good. When we get to know God more and more, we respond with joy and praise, and we want others to know Him too. What do you know about God that makes you want to praise Him?

Father God, You are worthy of our worship. We praise You because You are great! You want others to know how great You are. Amen.

THOUGHTS FOR DADDY

Why do we worship God? Have you ever thought about that? Does God need us to tell Him how great He is? Read Psalm 50:10–12. God needs nothing from us. Everything belongs to Him.

Instead, God commands our worship because He deserves it. He alone is perfect and holy. He alone holds all things in the universe together. When we know God, our right response is to worship Him. Worship reminds us what is true about God. It is an act of humble surrender to Him—on our knees or in our hearts—as our King. Why do you believe God is worthy of worship? What is your favorite way to worship God?

EVERY GOOD GIFT

Every good and perfect gift is from above,
coming down from the Father of lights,
who does not change like shifting shadows.
—James 1:17

Did you know that God loves to give us gifts? Does that surprise you? After all, I don't remember seeing a present that said "From God" under the Christmas tree or at your last birthday!

The Bible says that every good gift comes from God. Just look around you. What are some things you enjoy? Look at the flowers outside, the birds in the air, the pink clouds at sunset—it is all from God for us. But you might be thinking your favorite toy came from the store or your grandma made you a special blanket. People create these things from the materials that God put on the planet. All of God's good gifts remind us that He loves us and has not stopped thinking about us.

Father God, thank You for everything that we enjoy—animals, friends, toys, books, and more. Help us remember that You are the Giver of every good gift. Amen.

THOUGHTS FOR DADDY

There is every reason for us to live with gratitude to God. Every breath is from Him; every heartbeat is for Him; every pleasurable thing is a foretaste of our future with Him.

As Christians, we understand that every good and perfect gift is a blood-bought gift that can be traced back to the cross of Christ. Especially when things seem to be going wrong, let's count God's good gifts. Write down three things every day to thank God for. Spend time in prayer, praising Him for these good gifts that can often go unnoticed. Model a grateful heart to your children however you can. There is much to be thankful for!

98

ASK AWAY

Don't worry about anything, but in everything, through prayer and petition with thanksgiving, present your requests to God.
—Philippians 4:6

Have you ever noticed that God does not always give us what we ask for? Maybe you asked God for a pet, but we didn't get one. Maybe you asked God for another sibling, but that hasn't happened. How do you feel when God says no?

It's important to remember that God is our heavenly Father—that means He loves to give us things, but not necessarily everything we want. For example, I'm your earthly daddy, and I love giving you things. But if you ask for ice cream for breakfast every day, I will say no. The Bible says God wants us to ask Him for things, and He always will give the best answer.

Father God, You care about us and hear all our requests. Help us trust You to answer us and give us everything we need. Amen.

THOUGHTS FOR DADDY

When your child needs help reaching a shirt in his closet or wants a snack from the pantry, does he sit around thinking about it? No, he asks you for what he needs!

As adults, we often think we have to do everything on our own. Some of us even believe that's what it means to be an adult. But we mustn't hesitate to ask God for things. He loves providing for us. Read Matthew 7:11. When we ask God for what we need, He provides it according to His will, and He doesn't stop at the bare minimum. He gives us more than we can ask or think of. Remember that God sees the bigger picture. He gives what is best, even if it's not what we asked for.

99

PRAY, PRAY, PRAY

Pray constantly.
—1 Thessalonians 5:17

The Bible says we should pray constantly. That means to pray all the time! What else do we do constantly? Well, we breathe constantly. We blink constantly. We feel constantly. A person who prays constantly understands that she needs God all the time.

God loves to hear from us—not just at bedtime or before a meal, but many times every day. Some people believe that you can only pray a certain number of times per day, in particular places, or at specific times of day. But the Bible says we can pray all the time, no matter where we are! Praying constantly reminds us that we need God.

Father God, You love to hear from us.
Help us be quick to pray to You—when we
wake up, while we play, when we eat,
at bedtime, and anytime! Amen.

THOUGHTS FOR DADDY

"Daddy? Daddy? Daddy? Daddy! Daddy!" Your little one is probably relentless in the amount of attention he needs from you. This is a clear sign of his dependence on you. Are you relentless in your prayers to God?

God wants us to be in constant communication with Him; this is a sign of our dependence on Him. Throughout your day, offer short prayers: "Father, good morning"; "Give me patience"; "Jesus, help me!" Pour out your heart to Him on a long commute. Lead your family in prayer. Pray for family members and neighbors. Prayer is our lifeline to heaven, to the God of the universe, to the Lord who has saved us. What do you need to talk to Him about right now?

THANK YOU, GOD!

Give thanks to the LORD, for he is good;
his faithful love endures forever.
—*Psalm 118:29*

If someone gives you a gift, what do you say? "Thank you!" The Bible tells us that we should also say thank You to God because He gives us everything we have. Let's practice thanking God together. The more we practice, the easier thanking God becomes!

"Thank You, God, for flowers and animals and all of creation! Thank You for friends, family, and a place to live. God, thank You for food to eat." What else can we thank God for? We can say thank You to God because He is good and generous. Thanking God helps our hearts stay right with Him.

Father God, You are good! Thank You for this life You give us, and thank You especially for Jesus. When we start to become ungrateful, please show us! Amen.

THOUGHTS FOR DADDY

Look around. Does gratitude for what you have come easily to you? Are you thankful for simple things like your clothes, your car, your job, and your home? Or do you focus on what you don't have and feel dissatisfied and bitter?

The Bible speaks repeatedly of giving thanks to the Lord. If you struggle with discontentment, read 1 Timothy 6:6–8. As you grow in your faith, God can help you grow in gratitude. A thankful spirit is a generous, open, and inviting spirit. This is what you want to model to your child as you lead him or her. Spend time practicing gratitude through prayer and sharing what you're thankful for with others.

BIG BIBLE
WORDS FOR ME

BLESSED (adj). truly happy (pg. 104)

CHURCH (n). a group of people who follow Jesus meeting together to listen to God's Word, worship Him, and serve others (pg. 121, 132)

COMMUNITY (n). a group of people who work for the good of everyone in the group (pg. 121)

DISOBEDIENCE (n). breaking the rules—either God's rules or human rules (pg. 68)

ENEMY (n). a person who is mean to or hurts someone else (pg. 198)

FORGIVENESS (n). not staying mad at or getting back at someone for hurting you (pg. 77)

GENEROUS (adj). happy and eager to give to others (pg. 184)

GLORIFY (v). to bring honor to (pg. 143)

HEART (n). the part of ourselves that tells us how we feel, what we want, and what is right or wrong (pg. 94)

HOLY (adj). set apart (pg. 28)

HONEST (adj). speaking the truth (pg. 174)

HUMILITY (n). understanding that God is most important and that others are just as important as you (pg. 172)

MIRACLE (n). something only God can do (pg. 70)

NEIGHBOR (n). anyone God brings into your life (pg. 200)

PRAISE (v). to tell God how great He is (pg. 220)

PRAY (v). to talk to God (pg. 210)

PRIDE (n). the feeling or belief that you are the best or the most important (pg. 172)

PROMISE (n). telling someone that you will do a specific thing or that a certain thing will happen in the future (pg. 33)

PURPOSE (n). the reason for something to exist (pg. 143)

RESCUER (n). a person who helps us when we are in need (pg. 72)

SACRIFICIAL (adj). giving up something you have and love for someone else (pg. 196)

SIN (v). to make a wrong choice that goes against God (pg. 80)

TEMPT (v). to encourage someone to sin (pg. 96)

TRUSTWORTHY (adj). when what you say is what you do (pg. 176)

UNIQUE (adj). different from others (pg. 128)

WISDOM (n). the God-given ability to make good or right choices (pg. 166)

WORSHIP (n). celebrating the greatness of God in many ways (pg. 214)

DADDY AND ME MOMENTS

On these pages, record your favorite "daddy and me" moments from your devotional reading. What questions about God did your child ask you that you don't want to forget? What ideas did he or she have about God? Did you read the devotional in a special place or while eating a special treat once in a while? Record memorable moments so that you can look back in the future to rediscover your child's spiritual interests and what conversations you enjoyed together.